More Than Patriotism

More Than Patriotism
Canada at War 1914-1918

by Kathryn M. Bindon

Series Editor, Dr. Donald Swainson

A Personal Library
Publication, produced
exclusively for

Nelson

More Than Patriotism

940.4
Bin
C1

Personal Library
Publishers
Suite 539
17 Queen Street East
Toronto, Canada M5C 1P9

A Personal Library publication
produced exclusively for
Thomas Nelson & Sons (Canada) Limited
81 Curlew Drive, Don Mills, Canada
M3A 2R1

Publisher: Glenn Edward Witmer
Editor: Margaret MacDonald
Series Design: Jonathan Milne
Book Design: First Image
Composition: CompuScreen Typesetting Ltd.

Canadian Cataloguing in Publication Data

Bindon, Kathryn M., 1949-
  More than patriotism

Includes index.
ISBN 0-17-600770-9

1. European War, 1914-1918—Canada. I. Title.

D547.C2B55   940.4'0971   C79-094635-1

Printed and bound in Canada

Acknowledgements

The wealth of visual resources describing the First World War and Canada's role in it is immense; however, the task of assembling the present collection was made both possible and enjoyable with the generous aid and contributions of the staff of the National Photography Collection, Public Archives of Canada, especially Ms. G. Chatel. I should particularly like to thank Mr. H. Halliday and Mr. F. Azar for introducing me to the outstanding collection of paintings and drawings, too rarely displayed, held by the Canadian War Museum in Ottawa.

   The many original quotations reproduced here are taken from archival, official and newspaper sources, as well as from other published materials, most of which are listed in the further reading section. To those scholars, who through their studies of individuals or specific events detailed the military story of the First World War, I wish to express my respectful gratitude.

PREFACE

The flow of world history is punctuated by cataclysmic events. The conquests of Alexander the Great, the barbarian invasions, Charlemagne's unification of the West, the Thirty Years' War and the Napoleonic wars are examples of intensive military activity that altered the course of history, often for the worse.

World War I is another such example. The face of the world was modified by that incredible war; we are still very much dominated by its results. The Austro-Hungarian, German and Russian empires were destroyed; the British empire survived, but was shaken. The United States of America was revealed as a great world power, and the basis was laid for an attempt at American hegemony over the West. By shattering Czarist Russia, the war made possible the success of the Russian Revolution and the emergence of the Union of Soviet Socialist Republics as a great power.

Much more was involved than shifts in military and political strength. World War I produced profound social changes. Industrialization was given a powerful push forward; women were liberated to a hitherto undreamed of extent. Many areas of Europe were decimated, and millions of people killed and maimed. Virtually all governments increased their power. Income taxes became all but universal. Nationalism was stimulated to the extent that it became one of the dominant ideologies of the twentieth century.

Many Canadians fail to realize that Canada was a major participant in World War I. Britain, Russia, France and Canada carried the main burden of the Allied cause until the United States entered the war in 1917. Some 630,000 Canadians served in the Canadian Expeditionary Force and the Canadian Navy. Thousands more served in the British forces. 60,000 Canadians were killed and over 170,000 wounded in one way or another. Canadian public finance was revolutionized, and a huge industrial edifice was constructed. Some women were given the vote during the war, and thousands more gained experience in the workforce. Trade unionism and radicalism were strengthened by changes wrought by the war, and by the tens of thousands of soldiers who, after 1918-19, returned to Canada in search of the better world they had fought for in Europe.

World War I was also central to the evolution of Canadian foreign policy. In 1914 we entered the war automatically; Canada was at war the minute Britain declared war. By 1919 we were recognized as a nation that controlled her foreign policy as well as her internal affairs. This dramatic change of status did not just happen.

Canada earned recognition as a sovereign state by her massive military contribution, a contribution made clear to the world by brilliant participation in such battles as Ypres, Vimy Ridge, Passchendaele as well as the Liberation of Mons and March to the Rhine.

Tragically, World War I set off one of our classic quarrels between English-speaking and French-speaking Canadians. Sir Robert Borden's Conservative administration, although a coalition after 1917, was never a truly national government. It was essentially a government of and for English-speaking Canada; French Canadians retained a fierce loyalty to Sir Wilfrid Laurier until his death in 1919. Borden's government, representative of most English Canadian opinion, was committed to a major Canadian role in the war; French Canada had no such commitment and was opposed to some of the policies generated by the Tories' dour commitment. The crisis came over Union government, the election of 1917 and conscription. Although the Liberal party retained substantial strength - throughout Canada, the House of Commons elected in 1917 was dangerously balanced. The Liberals swept Quebec, but elected only twenty M.P.'s in English Canada; only two were elected in the four western provinces. Borden and his allies scored a stunning victory in English Canada, and were overwhelmingly rejected in Quebec. Conservatives were in serious trouble in Quebec long before 1917, but the events of that traumatic year had a lot to do with the veritable destruction of the Conservative Party in that crucial province. This basic fact has been one of the defining characteristics of the Canadian experience in the twentieth century.

We learn much by studying World War I. A government that was really representative of only one of our two historic language groups bound Canada to policies and commitments that were not acceptable to the entire nation. The resultant conflict threatened the very existence of this country. This book thus reveals much about the Canadian political process at the very highest level. It is also a social history. Professor Bindon takes us into the trenches with our foot soldiers. With them we relive the agony and horror of some of the greatest battles of modern history. World War I shaped much of the history of twentieth century Canada. *More Than Patriotism* enables us to experience the nature of the war, and to understand more fully its influence on Canadian development.

Donald Swainson
Garden Island, Ontario
July 8, 1979

INTRODUCTION

November 11 ... "In Flanders Fields" ... lapel poppies — faint reminders of the "War to end all Wars" into which Canada was drawn over sixty years ago. The events that took place in Europe during the summer months of 1914 initially appeared to have little to do with Canada and Canadians. The years between 1914 and 1918, however, were to test the North American colony's very roots: Canada would emerge from the Great War with a heightened national identity, a tradition of military excellence and a lasting international reputation.

The First World War was a time of paradox, of contradiction and of testing. The strategies and materiel of nineteenth-century warfare were welded to the inventions and ideas of twentieth-century military technology to produce a war in which the Cavalry and the Tank Corps, the aeroplane and the bayonet would play equally important parts. It was also a conflict in which the relatively humane traditions of past European warfare would yield to the horror of devastating new weapons and the cynicism of their masters on both sides.

Canada was totally involved in every facet of the War. In the trenches of the Western Front, Canadians earned the reputation of being an organized, disciplined and enormously effective fighting force. They also secured the right to fight under their own General Staff, an important step in Canada's gradual assumption of autonomy within the Empire. On the home front, Canada experienced a period of political and economic change that was worthy of pride but at the same time ridden with scandal. Unprecedented economic growth was coupled with increasingly divided politics, and the man who argued for a flexible, rational and yet patriotic war policy, Sir Wilfrid Laurier, was pushed aside by the excessive wartime zeal of his countrymen. Curiously, this same investment in "victory at all costs" was to permit Prime Minister Robert Borden and his Conservative and Anglophone Union Parties to ride out a series of scandals that both shocked the public and threatened Canadian efforts at the Front.

The years of conflict were so amazingly complex that it is quite possible to study any single detail of the War of 1914-1918 in great depth. A broader viewpoint is desirable, however, in order to recognize the relationships that existed between many of the events that took place. Notwithstanding, it is also too easy to look at the War solely in terms of grand strategy and international leadership. Beyond these aspects of military activity lie the men who fought and those who supported them at home. Since Canadians were involved mainly on the Western Front, it is on this sector that *More Than Patriotism* concentrates. While private cameras were banned at the Front, photographs by Canada's Official Photographers enable us to "see" the War as experienced by Canadian soldiers, recording forever his pride, fear, victory and loss.

"Raised by Patriotism ... Killed by Politics."

8

The Western Front, 1914-1918
Canadian Operations

The Battles of Ypres, April-May 1915
The Actions at Festubert and Givenchy, May-June 1915
The St. Éloi Craters, March-April 1916
The Battle of Mount Sorrel, 2-13 June 1916
The Battles of the Somme, July-November 1916
The Battle of Vimy Ridge, 9-12 April 1917
The Battles of the Scarpe, April-May 1917
The Capture of Hill 70, 15-25 August 1917
The Battle of Passchendaele, 26 October-10 November 1917
The Battle of Amiens, 8-11 August 1918
The Battle of Arras, 26 August-3 September 1918
The Canal du Nord and Cambrai, 27 September-11 October 1918
The Capture of Valenciennes, 1-2 November 1918

In the Summer of 1914, the philosophies, politics, militarisms and imperialisms of nineteenth-century Europe came together in a war for which no nation was prepared.

The roots of this conflict lay in the nineteenth century. In 1870, Germany had occupied Alsace-Lorraine, territory that was considered to be French. This was still an issue in 1914. As the century turned, the great armaments race was under way, most notably between the British and German navies. Both forces began building massive ships called "dreadnoughts" and matching each other's acquisitions ship for ship.

The armaments race was mirrored by a growth of nationalism.

Germany, buttressed by the ideas evolved throughout the nineteenth century by many of her philosophers, developed a sense of future role that, combined with militarism, proved fertile ground for the growth of aggressive sentiments.

The cousins who ruled Germany and Britain increasingly represented two conflicting world views.

Kaiser Wilhelm II

King George V

The potential for war had existed for over a decade:
The events that created it converged in little over a month.

June 28, 1914:
Archduke Franz Ferdinand, heir to the throne of Austria-Hungary, and his wife Sophie were assassinated by Serbian nationalists in Sarajevo. The shot was fired in the name of Bosnia-Herzegovina, a territory annexed to Austria-Hungary that some argued belonged to Serbia. The area, indeed the whole of the Balkan States, had been the scene of frequent troublesome demonstrations, and the Austrian government decided to investigate thoroughly the possibility that Serbian authorities had been involved in the murder plot.

July 28, 1914:
One month later, the Austro-Hungarian Empire declared war on Serbia, bringing into potential play an intricate network of European alliances and ententes that had been formulated in the years before 1914.

July 30, 1914:
Russia, as protector of the Balkans, mobilized for war against Austria-Hungary. This was of signal importance in that it prompted German involvement. When asked, Moltke, Chief of the German General Staff, responded that the Fatherland was in danger as a result of Russia's action.

July 31, 1914:
Germany, ally of Austria-Hungary, demanded immediate demobilization of Russian troops.

August 1, 1914:
Russia refused: Germany declared war on Russia.

August 2, 1914:
Germany demanded an unobstructed right of passage through neutral Belgium in order to implement her war plan. This was an offensive strategy that had been formulated by Schlieffen, Chief of the German General Staff from 1892 through 1906. The essential element of the plan was a decisive victory on the western (French) frontier to forestall the possibility of engagement on two frontiers. Russia's quick mobilization on Germany's eastern front was not according to the Schlieffen Plan, but the Germans decided to proceed with it anyway. Belgium, however, refused Germany's request for passage across her territory on the way to France.

13

August 3, 1914:
Schlieffen had been correct about one aspect of the events that would immediately precede the war: mobilization did, in fact, mean war. Without much attempt at a diplomatically acceptable rationale, Germany declared war on France and ignored Belgium's refusal of passage.

August 4, 1914:
Rushing to the aid of Belgium, Britain declared war on Germany on behalf of herself and her Empire. Although determined not to become involved in a conflict that could be described as a Balkan quarrel, Britain could not ignore the more bellicose actions of Germany with regard to Belgium and France.

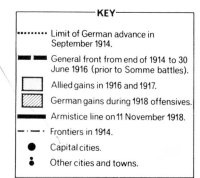

KEY

.... Limit of German advance in September 1914.

■■ ■■ General front from end of 1914 to 30 June 1916 (prior to Somme battles).

☐ Allied gains in 1916 and 1917.

▨ German gains during 1918 offensives.

■■■ Armistice line on 11 November 1918.

—·—· Frontiers in 1914.

● Capital cities.

⁝ Other cities and towns.

14

The First World War thus began almost in spite of the belligerents.

As the months passed, more nations joined one side or the other, until the line-up of allies included Japan, Italy, Bulgaria, Roumania, Britain and France, fighting against Germany, Austria-Hungary and Turkey. The conflict spread to various African colonies, the Dardanelles and the Middle East. But it was more a war of the Western Front, confined to Belgium, and France, than of the world. It was in these areas that most of the fighting, and the major decisions, took place.

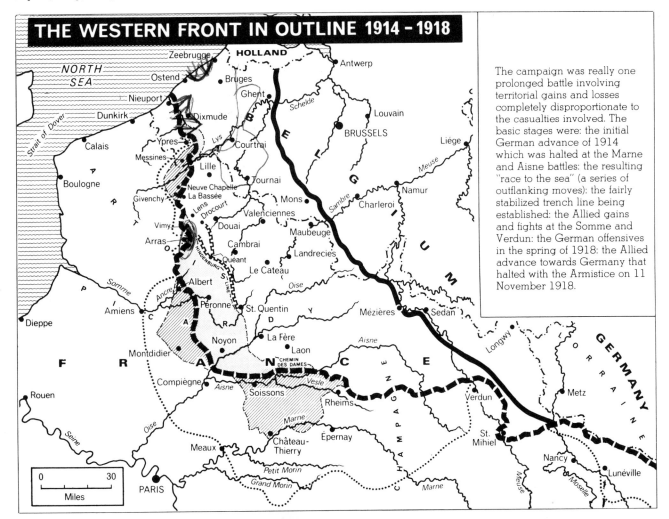

THE WESTERN FRONT IN OUTLINE 1914 - 1918

The campaign was really one prolonged battle involving territorial gains and losses completely disproportionate to the casualties involved. The basic stages were: the initial German advance of 1914 which was halted at the Marne and Aisne battles: the resulting "race to the sea" (a series of outflanking moves): the fairly stabilized trench line being established: the Allied gains and fights at the Somme and Verdun: the German offensives in the spring of 1918: the Allied advance towards Germany that halted with the Armistice on 11 November 1918.

NORTH SEA
Zeebrugge
HOLLAND
Antwerp
Ostend
Bruges
Nieuport
Ghent
Schelde
Louvain
Dixmude
BRUSSELS
Liège
Dunkirk
Strait of Dover
Calais
Ypres
Lys
Courtrai
Meuse
Messines
Lille
Tournai
Boulogne
Neuve Chapelle
Namur
Givenchy
La Bassée
Lens
Mons
Charleroi
Drocourt
Valenciennes
Sambre
Vimy
Douai
Maubeuge
Arras
Cambrai
HINDENBURG LINE
Quéant
Landrecies
Le Cateau
Somme
Ancre
Albert
Oise
Peronne
St. Quentin
Amiens
Dieppe
Noyon
La Fère
Laon
Aisne
Mézières
Sedan
Montdidier
CHEMIN DES DAMES
Compiègne
Aisne
Vesle
Soissons
Rheims
Verdun
Metz
Rouen
Seine
Oise
Marne
Épernay
St. Mihiel
Meaux
Château-Thierry
Petit Morin
Nancy
Lunéville
Grand Morin
Marne
Meuse
Moselle
PARIS
GERMANY
LORRAINE
BELGIUM
FRANCE
CHAMPAGNE
ARTOIS
PICARDY

0   30
Miles

On August 4, Canada was involved in this bewildering sequence of European events.

As a colony of Great Britain, still dependent in matters of international commitments, Canada found herself automatically included in Britain's declaration of war in 1914.

Canada's status with regard to British military involvements had been undergoing clarification since Confederation. After the commencement of the Boer War, this relationship had required additional definition. The Canadian commitment to the South African struggle amounted to the equipping of 2,000 volunteer troops, but the intention of the government was to be careful of Canadian military commitments to potential future conflicts:

"I claim for Canada this, that in the future Canada shall be at liberty to act or not to act, to interfere or not to interfere, to do just as she pleases, and that she shall reserve to herself the right to judge whether or not there is cause for her to act."

Prime Minister
Wilfrid Laurier,
February 5, 1900

Not until 1940, when Canada declared war against Germany in an independent action, would this status be actively proclaimed, but Laurier's insistence upon increasing autonomy was important in 1914 when Canada became a belligerent in what had appeared all along to be a purely European conflict.

Sir Wilfrid Laurier

Canada had a volunteer militia army in 1914.

Aldershot Camp, Nova Scotia, 1913

While the militia was originally under the control of a British Commander, after the Boer War this too was increasingly Canadianized. A Canadian General Staff was created to ensure internal control and direction of the forces, and the size of the establishment was dramatically increased.

In 1914, the Canadian military amounted to a permanent force of about 3,000 regulars, and a partially-trained volunteer militia force, of almost 60,000 men. Canada's population was close to 8,000,000 in 1914.

Camp Sewell, Manitoba

Militia, Kingston, Ontario

The decade of gradual change was important.

All of the efforts to increase the size and autonomy of Canada's military organization would prove of essential importance when Canada, only partially independent, was drawn into the European conflict on August 4 when Prime Minister Robert Laird Borden announced Canada's status as a joint-belligerent in the First World War.

Sir Robert Laird Borden

Nothing but patriotism answered his announcement.

The response of all Canadians was united and completely supportive. There was no question but that the colony would exert every effort in support of the Mother Country. But it was also important that Canada's automatic involvement be understood in terms of a national, not just Imperial, obligation.

"War is the one compelling fact; Peace is the one constructive hope. Not for the sake of War is Canada justified in involving America in the madness of European strife, and in sending tens of thousands of Canadian citizens to line up against citizens of Germany on battlefields in France and Belgium and on to Berlin. That were a national crime, an apostasy from Canada's national ideal, an outrage upon humanity of which only barbarians could be guilty. But for the sake of Peace, for conserving the honour and the integrity of Britain, for protecting the national rights and interests, even the very national existence of Belgium, and for making possible an enduring and a righteous peace for all the defenceless little peoples of Europe and of all the world, Canada is taking no more than its share of a free nation's burden in pledging to the full the strength of the Canadian people. For War, brutal, cruel, selfish, nothing but denial and refusal; for Peace, free, unchallenged, righteous, everything the people can do and the nation can give."

Editorial
Globe,
September 28, 1914

Leaving Toronto for Valcartier, 1914

The creation of an army was the immediate task.
Canada decided what kind of a commitment to make.

Valcartier Camp, Quebec

If Canadians were not allowed to make an independent decision about their involvement in this war, they did, according to Laurier's statement, possess the right to define the kind and extent of their contribution. By August 6, the Canadian government had agreed that her part would be a contingent of 25,000 men to be deployed as required.

Headquarters, 1st Division,
Valcartier Camp, Quebec

Cadet Camp at Long Branch,
Toronto

More than 33,000 men volunteered — the majority of them British born — and they were assembled at Valcartier Camp, near Quebec City, for organization and initial equipping.

Valcartier had been created especially to handle the new Canadian army. And it proved an exceptionally efficient operation, considering the newness of the whole experience.

The First Contingent, Canadian Expeditionary Force, left Gaspé Bay on October 3, 1914.

They arrived in Plymouth, England, in October, 1914 and proceeded to Salisbury Plain for additional training.

Canadian troops on Salisbury
Plain

Canadians at Plymouth Hoe,
October 20, 1914

This was an Imperial force.

Rumours that the Canadian Contingent would be led by the Canadian Minister of Militia and Defence, Sam Hughes, were contradicted by the news that Canadian troops would be at the complete disposal of the British War Office.

Sam Hughes protected the integrity of his force.

If he could not lead the Canadian Expeditionary Force personally, Hughes was determined that they would not lose their integrity and be broken up for use as reinforcements for British regular troops. One Canadian officer later recalled a meeting between Hughes and Lord Kitchener, British Secretary of War:

"Sir Sam marched up to Kitchener's desk. When he arrived at the desk Kitchener spoke up quickly and in a very stern voice said: 'Hughes, I see you have brought over a number of men from Canada; they are of course without training and this would apply to their officers. I have decided to divide them up among the British regiments; they will be of very little use to us as they are.' Sir Sam replied: 'Sir, do I understand you to say that you are going to break up these Canadian regiments that came over? Why, it will kill recruiting in Canada.' Kitchener answered: 'You have your orders, carry them out.' Sir Sam replied: 'I'll be damned if I will,' turned on his heel and marched out."

Canadian soldiers were discouraged from accepting commissions in the British army, and thus the colonial troops retained their military integrity and from the beginning considered themselves equal to the troops of other Allied nations.

Sam Hughes of Canada

Because they were under British control, there was confusion at home as to their deployment.

Arriving at Salisbury, fully equipped, 1914

Canadian troops were placed under the command of a British officer, Lieutenant-General E.A.H. Alderson. But it was some time before they were sent into the line in Europe, and the First Contingent passed the winter months of 1914 in extreme discomfort on Salisbury Plain. Chronically cold and wet, by January 1915 almost 1,000 Canadians had been hospitalized, including twenty reported cases of spinal meningitis which raised fears of the possibility of a serious epidemic.

It was a matter of training.

The British were intent upon ensuring that the troops from the Dominion were properly prepared for combat. More was required than simply an ability to shoot straight, and it was veterans of the South African War and former British regulars, formed into the Princess Patricia's Canadian Light Infantry, who first entered the line. Their first encounter in Ypres immediately established their reputation as fighting men:

"After being thinned down by a withering fire from the British trenches, those [Germans] who remained were astonished to hear a roar of voices, and to see a long line of slouch-hatted men in khaki rush forward to meet them, shouting 'For Canada and Old England.'"

Globe
January 16, 1915

In camp at Salisbury Plain, England

During the winter months of 1915, all Canadian troops were transported to France.

King George V and Queen Mary inspected the troops at Salisbury Plain while the Canadians cheered them. Under the watchful eye of Sam Hughes, the rest of the Contingent crossed the Channel and arrived at St. Nazaire on February 11, 1915.

Canadian soldiers break loose in a very unmilitary salute to the King on Salisbury Plain.

King George V, Queen Mary and Lord Kitchener inspect Canadian troops.

This was the first campaign.

But the annual entry into a new campaign, and into battles whose most significant results were casualties, and perhaps a few yards, would become familiar fare to Canadians at home. For now, there was still an unquestioning sense of honour involved in winning this war that was as much a Canadian struggle as the early Indian wars of New France.

As Sir John Hendrie, Lieutenant-Governor of Ontario, remarked in 1915: "The men of Canada fighting in France are fighting for Canada as much as if the battleground were the banks of the St. Lawrence."

Poster: Follow the example of Dollard des Ormeaux. Don't wait for the enemy — go out and meet him.

Canada continued to send men to the Western Front.

Troops in Victoria, B.C.

A Second Division landed in France in September, 1915.

The Third Division, which increased the establishment of the Canadian force to 500,000 men, was authorized in December 1915 and arrived in France early in 1916.

A Fourth Division joined the Canadian Corps in Europe in August, 1916, while a Fifth Division, raised in 1917, was used to reinforce the Canadian Corps in 1918.

Saskatoon's contribution to the Second Contingent, 1915

Training commenced in Canada.

Camp Borden, just north of Toronto, Ontario, was purchased to become Canada's equivalent of Aldershot, the British training centre. Capable of accommodating thousands of men, Borden became a major centre for training in many corps services.

Canada's Greatest Military Review. General Sam Hughes leads Canadian troops in three cheers for King George at the review at Camp Borden of 30,000 troops.

Signal training at the Exhibition Grounds, Toronto

Battles in Canada.

Humber Battle, Toronto, Ontario,
March 3, 1916

Mock battles, along with exercises and reviews, were an important component of the training of Canadian troops.

The Exhibition Grounds, Toronto, Ontario, February 24, 1917

Battle of High Park, Toronto, Ontario, April 7, 1916

The final phase of meeting the standards of this war was concluded in Britain.

Church Service for Canadian Troops at Stonehenge, Salisbury Plain

The need for relocation before completion of training was endorsed by Canadian authorities, who recognized that the North American climate, harvest leave, and the proximity of home and family made efficient training in Canada almost impossible. Thus men were transported to England as soon after enlistment as possible, and their adjustment to the military life continued in new, and sometimes strange, surroundings. The problems of Salisbury did not repeat themselves. Canadians were kept in quarantine in Segregation Camps for at least twenty-eight days to solve the problem of disease. Permanent barracks were supplied for all troops.

Canadians were eager to get to the war, and anxious about what they would find upon arrival.

Recruits carrying bedding in the Exhibition Grounds, November 1914

From August 4, 1914 to November 15, 1918, 465,984 Canadians volunteered for service. Fifty-one per cent of these men were native-born Canadians, the majority of the rest were British-born.

All were fighting for King and Country.

This was a war of hideous inventions.

The battle of Ypres, during April and May of 1915, exposed Allied soldiers to one of the new horrors of this war: poisonous gas. Canadians were among the first to confront the Germans' new offensive weapon, and one observer reported the attack:

"The strong, northeast wind, which was blowing from the enemy's lines across the French trenches, became charged with a sickening, suffocating odour, which we recognized as proceeding from some form of poisonous gas. The smoke moved like a vivid green wall some four feet in height for several hundred yards and extending to within 200 yards of our extreme left. Gradually it rose higher and obscured the view."

A glance at the weather vane tells whether a gas alert is on or off.

Canadians buying oranges and chewing gum from French children who carry their gas masks in canvas bags

The British Commander, Field Marshall Sir John French, remarked that the Germans seemed well prepared and supplied with this gas, indication of "long and deliberate preparation for the employment of devices contrary to the terms of The Hague Convention, to which the enemy subscribed." Interestingly, the Germans had preceded their introduction of this weapon by public statements that the Allies were in fact using such gases.

The introduction of this weapon led to a new piece of standard equipment—for soldiers and civilians alike—and people on the Western Front began to regard a gas mask as simply another piece of clothing.

Both sides began to manufacture gas, and the chemicals became deadlier.

One of the many varieties of gas masks in use on the Western Front. This is a German variation without eye protection captured in 1917.

Gas projectors used by Canadians during advance on Lens, September, 1917

The first gas had been Citran gas, which the Germans produced in the trenches. This compound killed through inducing an acute bronchitis that ultimately asphyxiated the soldier, a process that often stretched out over a number of days. But each year the chemicals and the method of launching them became more sophisticated, until by 1918 both enemy and Allies were employing vapours that were vastly more devastating. The Allied forces demonstrated, in view of King George, a combination of deadly gas and liquid fire (essentially burning oil projected in successive shots across the disputed field) in the summer of 1917.

The Germans developed "mustard gas."

Mustard gas burns

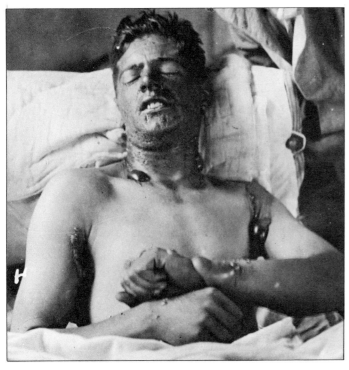

Massive amounts of this deadly gas, which hung in the immediate atmosphere for two to four days, were used by the Germans in the last campaigns of 1917 and 1918. One attack of forty-eight hours duration consumed 7,000 tons of mustard gas.

One Canadian newspaper explained the new substance to its readers:

"The name was given by the Tommies, for no 'mustard' is used in its composition. A drop of it on the sleeve penetrates and causes a blister like mustard, involving a severe burn and great swelling. It is so innocent in appearance and inoffensive in smell that the soldiers were not on guard against it, and even the masks when worn were powerless against an atmosphere full of the drug. The gas seldom kills outright, but its effects have shown it to be the most dangerous of all the gasses used by the Germans."

Globe
August 1, 1918

Gas was, however, as dangerous for its employer as for its object: any shift in the wind could turn the deadly substance back on those who launched it, and its after-life poisoned the atmosphere of many battlefields for days.

41

Ypres, then, was Canada's baptism by fire.

The ghastly geography of this conflict would become a familiar sight over the next three years, but in 1915 the devastated land and tangled bodies of this "new Pompeii" still represented the means to moral victory. Moreover, it was here that the building of a twentieth-century Candian military reputation was begun.

F.M. Armington 8012: The wounded promenade

At home, war was fought with words.

Propaganda was an important part of the total war effort. The Hun and the Boche were familiar targets of attack.

These European warriors were noted in North America for their stupidity, their brutality and their dishonesty.

"KNIGHTS OF THE AIR"

LOOK HINDENBURG ! MY GERMAN HEROES !

43

There was a North American front to be protected, too.

The threat of German spys operating in the neutral United States created numerous incidents of either real or perceived internal threats. A plot to blow up the Welland Canal was discovered in New York City; and one to blow up factories in Windsor was uncovered in Detroit. On the evening of February 13, 1915, the Chief of Police of Brockville, Ontario, warned Ottawa authorities that three unidentified planes had taken off from a field in upper New York State and were heading for Ottawa. A total black out of the capital was immediately ordered, but the planes never appeared.

In 1916, poor Hans Schmidt of Toledo, Ohio, marched into Windsor, Ontario, looking for the forces of the Kaiser that he had heard were assembling in Canada. To allay growing fears of alien unrest, the Minister of Militia, Sam Hughes, announced that he had investigated these threats and decided that aliens resident in Canada were "intensely loyal" — it was only a few Germans resident in the United States who were trying to stir up trouble.

Fire in the Parliament buildings.

Exterior wall of East Wing,
Centre Block, Parliament Hill

In February, 1916, a fire destroyed a large part of the Canadian Parliament buildings. Initially the disaster was reported to be the work of German incendiaries, and a report from the Providence *Journal* that it had been informed by employees of the German Embassy in Washington that plans to attack the Parliament buildings, Rideau Hall and munitions plants were being put into motion, seemed to support this idea. Within days, however, Ottawa officials had declared the fire to have been caused accidentally and spread through natural causes, and the rumours that this had been an enemy attack were stopped.

The Hun was compared to the Iroquois.

M.895.

This Canadian symbol of brutality in warfare was frequently used, and the reporting of atrocities committed by German soldiers served to increase Canada's determination to maintain her commitment. Germans were reported as having beaten wounded British soldiers to death in their frustration at being defeated, and the story of the "Crucified Canadian" — one or more Canadian soldiers nailed or bayoneted to makeshift crosses at various points on the Western Front — surfaced in numerous variations.

"Canada's Golgotha"

There were enough real horrors to provoke hatred.

Canadian sentiments were very pro-British in this war. Canadians were incensed at the execution of nurse Edith Cavell. Although British, nurse Cavell became a powerful symbol for Canadians, who perceived her suffering to be additional cause for steadfastness.

Cavell herself had recognized the fallacy of these feelings, for shortly before her death she said: "But this I would say, standing as I do in view of God and eternity, I realize that patriotism is not enough. I must have no hatred or bitterness towards anyone."

Canadians were especially incensed by attacks on hospitals.

Canadian hospital at Étaples,
France, after being bombed by
German airmen

What appeared to be the deliberate bombing of a Canadian hospital at Étaples, France, caused the death of Canadian men and women. And a Canadian hospital ship, the *Llandovery Castle,* was torpedoed on its return to Europe when it was carrying Canadian medical personnel. As one observer remarked:

"The killing of men in battle or in their billets behind the Front is war. The bombing of hospitals and the torpedoing of hospital ships is premeditated murder, for the men who take part in these devilish atrocities know that some at least of their victims must be the noble women who wear the brassard of the Red Cross."

Without warning, in May, 1915, the passenger liner *Lusitania* was torpedoed.

German Commemorative Lusitania Medal 1915, symbol of brutality. One side — passengers buying tickets from death. Caption "Geschaft Uber Alles."

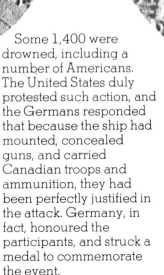

German commemorative Lusitania Medal, 1915. Obverse: Lusitania sinking with caption "Keine Bann Ware."

Some 1,400 were drowned, including a number of Americans. The United States duly protested such action, and the Germans responded that because the ship had mounted, concealed guns, and carried Canadian troops and ammunition, they had been perfectly justified in the attack. Germany, in fact, honoured the participants, and struck a medal to commemorate the event.

For Canadians, this attitude symbolized her savagery, brutality and lack of humanity — indeed, if not defeated, Germany would sink civilization without warning.

A greeting left by German troops: "God strafe England."

Europe's fate was blamed on the Germans as well.

German destruction of houses

Thanksgiving Service
celebrated in Cambrai
Cathedral, October 13, 1918

The barbarism and
stupidity of the Hun was
constantly evident. The
wanton destruction of
land and property
increased Germany's
debt to civilization.

By the end of 1915, it was obvious that this was a new kind of war.

On the Western Front, the fallacy of the offensive as a decisive strategy became inescapable in the defensive, static entrenchment of both sides along the Western Front.

"None can examine what, for want of a better name, is called the Front of this amazing war without realizing the truth of what has been so often said, that it is a war almost without a front. As one approaches from a distance the actual point of contact between the opposing forces, one is struck ever more and more by the immense numbers which are converging, as it seems, for some great military purpose, but the nearer the Front is approached the more completely does all that is spectacular disappear, until finally the flower of the youth of Europe disappears and is swallowed by immense but barely visible lines of field fortifications."

Official Canadian Recorder, March, 1915

The trench became home for many Canadian troops.

Every aspect of the soldier's life was regulated by this existence underground.

A battered trench

Canadians digging trenches

At the best of times,
soldiers dealt with lice,
rats, and snipers.

A German sniper's mask made
of half-inch Krupp steel

Tree overlooking Allied trenches
used by German snipers, April,
1917

Canadian soldier picking lice
out of his shirt

German sniping post and rifle

A little music outside the dug-out

Unidentified Canadian soldier in
the trenches, France, 1915

A quiet game at the Front

But there was always a way to adjust:

"One is impressed with the curious atmosphere of comradeship in the trenches. Here was absolute cheerfulness, even occasional hilarity, but all with an undertone of steadfastness, resolution and preparedness for instant and absolutely unselfish action in the great cause."

Britton R. Cooke,
September 17, 1915

Or a way to beat the snipers.

Dummy heads were used to
confuse German snipers.

At other times, there was no choice.

Canadians take some air after Germans strafe their dug-out.

A familiar sight at the front — writing the name on the cross

An attack was total, and if the military gain was often small, the military involvement was massive.

"The air is full of shells of all calibres, the small ones whistling and shrieking and the heaviest falling silently, followed by a terrific explosion which perforates even the padded eardrums, so that a thin trickle of blood down the neck bears witness that the man is stricken stone-deaf. The solid ground rocks like an express at full speed, and the only comparison possible is to a volcano in eruption with incessant shudder of earthworks pelting hail or rocks."

Special Correspondent to *Globe*, April 15, 1916

Through it all, Canadians in the trenches remained healthy, and even cheerful.

Morning on the battlefield

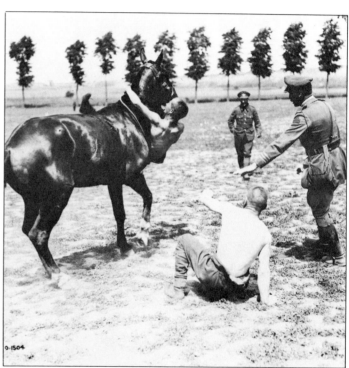

Wrestling on horseback behind the lines

Any time for relaxation or exercise was used to the full by Canadians at the Front who accommodated themselves to the conditions of the trench in leisure as well as military activities.

"The Dumbells" Concert Party.
Big Beauty Chorus, Marie and
the Boys. Groups for theatrical
entertainment were often formed
within Corps. The Dumbells
were one of the most famous,
and their vaudevillian antics
were, and still are, remembered
by many Canadians.

The entire cast of the "Dumbells"
in the closing number of the
show

The Canadian Corps was a massive organization of men, machines and animals.

The Lewis gun

A part of the First British Army, the Canadian Corps consisted of four Divisions and Corps Troops which in turn were organized into a number of arms that together supported, maintained, supplied and engaged the war on the Western Front.

The Infantry and the Artillery were involved in the first aspects of the attack: Artillery to bombard, cut the barbed wire in No Man's Land and prepare the ground for the advance of the Infantry.

A heavy howitzer on the Somme

Bridges and railways were important aspects of this new war.

Engineers built and repaired roads and bridges and the Railway Corps satisfied a basic need of this defensive war: the fast movement of reinforcements and supplies to the front lines.

Medical services came into their own after the battle.

Field and stationary hospitals were established all over the Front. Casualty clearing stations, and ambulance services were essential aspects of this Corps.

Hospital Unit on the march

Bringing out the wounded. A casualty clearing station near the line.

Ordnance services provided the means for this war.

A limited quantity of munitions were kept on the Front line, and Ordnance Corps were responsible for maintaining the supply.

Communications were essential.

Canadian Artillery observation
post in reserve line

Both the newest and
the oldest means of
communication were
employed in this war that
depended upon
techniques of the
nineteenth century and
inventions of the
twentieth.

Tying the message to the bird
before despatching it. His
Majesty's Pigeon Service, 1917.

Unable to ride his cycle
through the mud caused by the
recent storm, a Canadian
messenger carries his "horse."

Camouflaged observation post
on the Western Front

Telephone testing station at the
Front

An emergency telephone post
behind the line

Horses were as important as mechanized transport.

Over 24,000 horses were in service on the Western Front during the war. The Cavalry distinguished itself in numerous battles, and horses were essential to transport.

(No. 8224) Siberian Battery Exercising with Gun Limbers at Petawawa Camp. Watercolour by C.W. Jefferys

W. JEFFERYS

71

The Veterinary Service
was kept busy
ministering to these
equine soldiers who were
often caught in the fire of
battle.

The Forestry Corps.

When Britain experienced shortages of timber due to the curtailment of supplies from Europe, Canada was asked to provide a Corps of men who could provide timber from Britain's forests.

The Foresters were involved in lumber operations in France as well — both to harvest timber and to cut down and clean up damaged forests, of which there were many by 1918.

Voluntary citizens' organizations also supported the soldier at the Front.

Funded by campaigns for financial support carried out annually at home, various volunteer and religious organizations provided amenities for soldiers at the Front. As one Y.M.C.A. request for contributions pointed out, the simple pleasures were magnified in their importance to men in war.

JUST AN ORDINARY CUP OF COFFEE! SURELY NOTHING COULD BE MORE COMMONPLACE TO YOU. BUT — To wounded, broken and exhausted Canadian men staggering out of a furnace of shells . . . with nerves torn to pieces, that little refreshment in the moment of crisis — who can measure its signifi-cance? For it may mean life itself!

Canadians being given hot teas at Soup Kitchen within a quarter of a mile of the Front line

1916 was much like 1915.

About March 16, 1916. Trench mortar ready to go over to Fritz. Canadian trench mortar battery wearing shrapnel helmets.

For Canadians on the Western Front, the active campaign of 1916 began with an engagement at St. Éloi and a new piece of personal equipment.

The presence of snipers and the constant shelling of No Man's Land prompted the introduction of a steel shrapnel helmet to replace the slouch hat worn through 1915.

The engagement of St. Éloi resulted in small gains, but Canadian casualties amounted to some 1,300. These figures would increase — in numbers and familiarity — with each battle fought.

Canadian soldiers threw their rifles away during 1916.

Originally equipped with the Ross rifle, a domestic manufacture, Canadian troops replaced it with the British Lee Enfield whenever possible. The Ross was a target rifle and tended to jam under fire. From the beginning, this equipment had been criticized by the British commanders, who were treated to some of Sam Hughes' invective for their audacity. The Ross rifle had been one of his personal projects, and Hughes, of course, insisted that the Ross was a superior weapon, aptly suited to the demands of this conflict.

It was the Canadian soldier, however, who made the final decision. Whenever possible, a Ross was left in the mud, a Lee Enfield was picked up.

Ross rifle

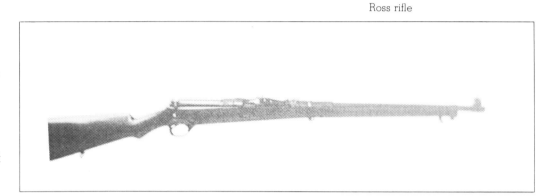

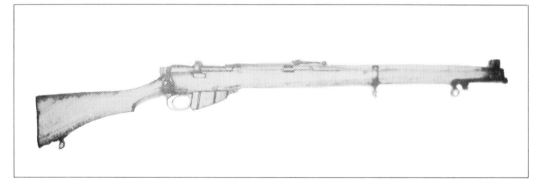

Lee Enfield rifle

Only once in this war were Canadian heavy guns captured.

During the Battle of Mount Sorrel, 2-13 June, 1916, two Canadian gun emplacements in Sanctuary Wood were lost to the Germans. Both were recovered, however, before the battle ended.

Hills were important on the Western Front — for advantage of height meant tactical superiority — and during this battle the Canadians recaptured three heights from the Germans.

Mount Sorrel cost the Canadians 8,000 casualties.

The two Canadian gun emplacements in Sanctuary Wood captured, for a short while, by the Germans

The battles never really ended.

Unexploded British two-inch trench mortar bomb lying in No Man's Land

While major engagements would end and troops might be moved from one location to another, No Man's Land was a constant, unchanging reminder of this war.

Life was constantly threatened by trench mortars, shrapnel, mines, duds and trench failures. And these threats never changed.

The battlefield after a Canadian charge

The Battle of the Somme was the disaster of 1916.

Sir Douglas Haig meets officers of the Second Canadian Division.

Canadians were moved from Ypres to the Somme to take part in this futile offensive. The responsibility of the Generals, who misjudged the situation seriously, was great. Sir Douglas Haig, who had assumed Command of the British Forces in Europe from Sir John French, was determined to mark the change with a victory.

Instead, Haig was responsible for one of the costliest encounters of the First World War.

a

Perforated sheet for Will from Pay Book of Reg.

No. 629885

Name *Thomas McGechie*

Unit *47th Batt*

Military Will.

*In the event of my
death I give the whole
of my property and effects
to my mother Mrs.*

*Thomas McGechie
2 North St.
Bathgate
Scotland*

Signature *Thomas McGechie*

Rank and Regt. *Pte 47th Batt*

Date *April 13 1916*

Military will of Canadian Private
Thomas McGechie

In one day — July 1 — 57,500 men were killed, wounded or reported missing.

Heavy howitzer in action

Shells of 15 inches are
unwelcome presents from
Canada to Germany

Over a period of five
months, only six miles
were gained. Canadian
casualties in the Somme
numbered 24,000. But
their reputation as soldiers
was underscored.

Courcelette was a major Canadian victory of the Somme offensive.

War Correspondent Philip Gibbs reported:

"The Canadians have gained great glory by their attack. The finely organized French-Canadians went away like wolves hunting. Though swept by machine guns, and meeting stubborn defence, they carried a stronghold and captured hundreds of prisoners. The full story of the Canadian victory will thrill the great Dominion like a heroic song. They were careless of death, so that they might win."

As the Somme ended, the Allies experienced some organizational changes on the home front.

Britain found itself with a new Prime Minister, as David Lloyd George replaced Herbert Asquith at the head of a coalition Cabinet. Lloyd George would prove a more demanding politician when it came to the Dominion's commitment.

Back in Ottawa, Sam Hughes resigned.

As soon as a Conservative government was assured, following the election of 1911, Hughes had approached Borden for confirmation of his Cabinet rank. Discrediting his political enemies as those who had also attempted to replace Borden as leader of the Conservative party, Hughes wrote of his qualifications for a Cabinet post:

In your coming Cabinet operations difficulties may from time to time arise. It strikes me that it might be that again, my tact, firmness and judgement might come in to help matters along.

"My military record is open — and will bear comparison with any. Sir Fred [Borden-Liberal Minister of Militia and Defence] himself has always done me the credit of saying that the vast majority of the democratic and effective changes are due to my suggestions. . . .

In my walks through life easy management of men has ever been one of my chief characteristics — and I get the name of bringing success and good luck to a cause."

Borden appointed Sam Hughes, who had in fact proved his stalwartness as a party man, to be Minister of Militia and Defence.

Hughes was the paradoxical Canadian hero of the early years of this war. While not of a heroic moral cast — his involvement in the munitions scandal was extremely uncomfortable for Canadians — Hughes was the driving force behind the success of the Canadian Expeditionary Force.

In 1915 he was knighted for his service to the Empire, and he never stopped fighting for his men at the Front.

Sam Hughes visiting the Front. Stepping off a torpedo boat.

His aggressive nature proved divisive at home, however.

In November, 1916, Borden requested and received Hughes' resignation. The question was one of overstepping the bounds of his authority, and while Sir Sam replied that it was all nonsense, Borden had his way.

But through the misguided plans and scandals, Hughes stood out as the one member of the Canadian government who had been willing to deal honestly — and impolitely — with British commanders who assumed an automatic superiority over the colonials. As one Canadian officer described him:

"Sam Hughes was the father and the mother of that formation which we sent overseas at the beginning of the First World War. Without Sam Hughes it never would have gone. Although there were many features about him of which I could not approve, I consider Sam the biggest single contribution Canada made to that war . . . Like many soldiers since then, he was a good actor. You saw him all the time. He was a picturesque figure and he played his part. Always on a horse, always picturesque, always in complete command of the whole thing."

Hughes wore his khaki uniform in Parliament, and his arrogance wherever he went.

Hughes was replaced by Sir Edward Kemp, who also became the Overseas Minister of Militia, a post newly created to reduce problems of communicating across the Atlantic. This post had originally been filled by Sir George Perley, Acting High Commissioner in London.

Major-General Sir Sam Hughes on board *H.M.S. Tartar* en route to France

Canada wanted more control.

Sir Robert Borden, General
Smuts and Sir George Halsey
Perley among others at the
Imperial War Conference, 1917

Borden demanded
more authority in Imperial
planning and, after the
stupidity of the campaign
and subsequent loss of the
Somme, Andrew Bonar
Law, Secretary of State for
the Colonies in Lloyd
George's coalition
Cabinet, agreed. As a
result of the sacrifice and
integrity of Canadian
troops at the Front, as well
as the need to rationalize
communications and
discussion of planning,
the Imperial War Cabinet
was formed early in 1917.
This was another stage in
the recognition of
Canada's right to military
autonomy.

The war at sea was between Britain and Germany.

The battle cruiser Hindenburg as she appeared at Scapa Flow, after the scuttling of the German Fleet, June 21, 1919

A small part of the British Fleet at anchor in the Firth of Forth

Both powers had anticipated a great naval showdown between their dreadnoughts, but the battle to decide who would finally rule the seas was not settled by any naval engagement. After the Peace, the German Fleet was scuttled — and the naval hegemony of Britain assured, at least for a while.

Canada's Navy, Canso, Nova
Scotia

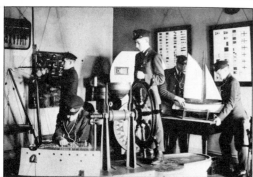

Students at the Royal Naval
College, Halifax, Nova Scotia,
1914

The Canadian Navy in 1914 consisted of two training vessels, the *Niobe* and the *Rainbow*. Establishment was less than 350 officers and men. Laurier's attempt to create a Canadian Navy in 1910 had been defeated by a coalition of the Conservatives, who argued that a colonial navy would be a threat to Imperial unity, and nationalists, who insisted that possession of a navy would involve Canada in Imperial wars.

The policy suggested by the new Conservative government was the transfer of $35,000,000 to the British Admiralty for the purchase of three dreadnoughts that would be considered Canadian ships — although at the disposal of the British Navy. Borden presented this policy as an important step in Canada's struggle for autonomy in external affairs, but the Naval Bill was rejected by the Senate.

In August 1914, Canada purchased two submarines from the United States.

Control of the Canadian Navy was offered to Great Britain, but the Admiralty, secure in their naval status, expressed only disinterest. As the war progressed, however, Canada and its navy became more important as a supplier of coastal patrol ships — usually anti-submarine trawlers — and men for the Royal Navy.

(No. 8367) Canadian Destroyers at Sea. Black chalk by Arthur Lismer

There were new weapons at sea.

The decisive weapon at sea was the submarine more than the dreadnought. Germany's initial superiority in this weapon was compounded by the nature of submarine warfare: no warnings were given and no survivors were picked up. The impact of the U-Boat was thus exaggerated in its effectiveness as an offensive weapon.

The Germans used their subs for purposes of commercial blocade as well as naval war, and the United States frequently complained that this employment was illegal in terms of international agreements regarding the freedom of the seas. Such complaints of commercial interference evoked no more response than the remonstrations about the sinking of the *Lusitania*.

German Submarine N97 and NSS Tug *Iroquois* at dock at foot of Yonge Street, June 11, 1919

German submarines threatened Canadian coastal waters, and the appearance of these underwater unknowns prompted Canadians to lament their lack of Naval power.

By 1918, Lloyd George was assuring the Allies that they were building ships faster than the Germans could sink them and sinking submarines faster than the Germans could build them. The idea was that the weight of the Allied effort could overcome this new menace.

And the propaganda value of the submarine was enormous — for its methods of attack were symbolic of the immorality and lack of courage of the German military generally.

Dogfight

There was also a war in the air on the Western Front. Initially used for reconaissance, the aeroplane became a decisive instrument of combat during this period. Small encounters between aerial observation pilots prompted the arming of aircraft, and the numbers of planes in a group multiplied until a new active arm had evolved and established itself as a permanent aspect of twentieth-century warfare.

Artillery Observation Training:
Learning to spot from the sky

(No. 8651) War in the Air. Oil
on canvas by C.R.W. Nevinson

Curtiss JN-4 gun installation and
R.F.C. gunner

German aeroplane which nose-
dived

Between 1911 and 1914, attempts to establish a Canadian Air Force had proved unsuccessful. In September, 1914, however, one aeroplane was purchased, and the Canadian Aviation Corps, which consisted of three men, went over to Britain as part of the First Contingent. It was never put to the test, and the Corps was disbanded in May 1915.

Canadians served with the Royal Flying Corps and the Royal Naval Air Service, which in April 1918 became the Royal Air Force, where the Canadians distinguished themselves as airmen. Unlike the Canadian involvement in the Royal Navy, which was thoroughly British and quite fully established, participation in the Royal Air Force provided a foundation for the formation of a Canadian Air arm.

Canada had its heroes in the air.

W.G. Barker and W.A. "Billy" Bishop both won Victoria Crosses for their missions.

Bishop had won a Victoria Cross for a solo encounter near Cambrai. He attacked a German airfield and engaged the fighters, destroying three before his ammunition ran out. His own plane was seriously damaged by ground fire.

Barker was awarded a Victoria Cross for an encounter in which he was attacked by sixty enemy Fokker planes. He destroyed four German planes, which raised his total number of victories to fifty, and returned, wounded, to crash-land within British lines.

H.R.H. The Prince of Wales and Lt. Col. W.G. Barker, V.C. preparing for flight in Sopwith 'Gnu' aircraft. Mr. T.O.M. Sopwith at left.

Canadians helped build the first rules of military aviation.

A model F5 Flying Boat being built in Toronto. It took three months to complete.

The newness of the arm was apparent in the discussion of inclusion of parachutes as official equipment. As late as August 1918 this piece of equipment which had proved successful in experimental tests was being suggested as a sensible precaution against accident or enemy fire. The process of reducing the vulnerability of the pilot was constant — and not always successful for the men who flew and fought in these fragile inventions.

The craft itself was continually being improved. Designs and armament were frequently redrafted or changed, and months were spent in producing planes — many of which were built in Canadian factories.

Putting on parachutes —
experimental equipment

This war marked the evolution of the Royal Canadian Air Force.

Although it was not until February, 1923, that the Royal Canadian Air Force was officially designated as such, over 20,000 Canadians participated in the R.A.F. Their official repatriation began immediately after the Peace, and a grant of equipment — including 40 German aeroplanes — by the Air Ministry of Great Britain helped the Air Force in peacetime.

There were new arms in the air, also.

An Allied rigid airship

A kite balloon being readied for an observation flight, 1916

The Germans used Zeppelins, huge rigid airships, to attack English towns and at first inflicted serious damage. These long, oval shaped vessels could carry up to two tons of bombs, and Zeppelin raids became another symbol of German barbarism in that they were attacks on women and children.

The Zeppelin gradually disappeared as a major menace: they were too easily destroyed, and proved more valuable for reconaissance than attack. The Allies comforted themselves that this German strategy had been a costly failure.

101

The war did not end in 1916.

29th Infantry Battalion advancing over "No Man's Land" through German barbed wire and heavy fire, Vimy Ridge

In spite of all hopes, a new year of war opened for Canadian troops with the Vimy Ridge campaign of April, 1917.

An effective artillery barrage caught the Germans unawares.

Between 9 and 12 April, the Canadians achieved an outstanding victory at a cost of 10,602 casualties.

102

German machine gun emplace-
ment taken during Vimy Ridge

This was the first totally
Canadian victory, in that
all four Divisions were
employed to dislodge the
Germans from three lines
of trenches (established in
1914), which were
heavily defended by
barbed wire
emplacements and
104 concrete redoubts.

If at all possible, captured guns were turned on their original owners.

Two German Howitzers, captured on Vimy Ridge by the Canadians, were turned against their original owners.

At Vimy, 54 guns, 104 trench mortars and 124 machine guns were captured — and such souvenirs of war were always assessed for their usefulness — either in the field or as salvage, or for experimental purpose.

105

Even individual trophies were included.

Carrying German spiked
helmets out of a captured dug-
out

Every soldier had
personal trophies, but if
they were of any possible
use, even these artifacts
were contributed to the
general war effort.
    There was no resource
that could be wasted in
war.

Canadian Corps Tramway men
reading Salvage Notice Board

107

Prisoners of war were taken in massive numbers.

Vimy alone produced 4,000 German prisoners of war, and these numbers were small in terms of those taken in battles during 1918.

During the attack, prisoners were placed in temporary cages. After, they were transferred to the rear cage, while waiting to be turned over to the authorities for final disposition.

German prisoners of war captured by the Canadians

There was often no time for such distinctions.

A wounded Canadian leads in a Bosche whose nerves have been shattered during the Allied advance on Hill 70.

It was not always practical to follow such regulations, and prisoners of war frequently served as stretcher bearers or aides during the battle.

Everyone hated the Hun —
But it was more difficult to despise the individual German.

Life at the Front was reduced to common physical denominators that evoked sympathy for their counterparts among the soldiers.

There was also an element of sympathy for the Germans who were being led astray by immoral and calculating leaders.

(No. 8656) Hans and Fritz.
Lithograph by C.R.W. Nevinson

A wounded Canadian and a wounded German light up after the Battle of Passchendaele, November, 1917.

C.3757

Canadian prisoners of war were interned in Germany and Switzerland.

Hockey team among Canadians interned in Switzerland

On the Western Front, 3,747 POWs were identified by the government. Of these, 301 died, 100 escaped and 438 were repatriated under agreements made between Germany and Britain, before the Armistice.

Canadians were employed in labour camps in Germany, but there were not many complaints of unjust treatment.

Canadian soldiers became "Byng Boys" when command was given to Sir Julian Byng in 1916.

While he was an Officer of the Imperial Forces, Sir Julian Byng was a popular commander with Canadian troops. Thus it was a sad day when the announcement was received that Byng was being replaced.

Lt. General Sir Julian Byng, General Officer Commanding, Canadian Corps, May, 1917

But for the first time, a Canadian was fully in charge of Canadian troops.

On June 23, 1917, Lieutenant-General Sir Arthur Currie assumed command of Canadian troops in Europe. Currie's background as a civilian had been in teaching and banking, and his military experience was traditionally Canadian — he had risen through the ranks of the militia.

With the First Canadian Contingent when it landed in 1915, Curie had achieved a distinguished battle record and had been honoured by Allied leaders for his military achievements.

General Currie, Commander of Canadian troops in Europe

Currie's appointment was popular with the troops.

The King, General Currie and General Horne at Vimy Ridge

But his reputation among the politicians at home was less than glowing. A Canadian Commander was expected to be co-operative — but Currie's main concern was the Canadian Corps whose needs were often in conflict with those of Conservative politicians in Ottawa.

Currie did not hesitate to criticize leaders (political or military) if he felt there was justification. And he adamantly refused to comply with Borden's demands for pro-conscriptionist communiqués to support the government in the 1917 election campaign. As he wrote to one Member of Parliament in 1917:

"I am glad to note that you are exerting all your influence to keep the Corps at full strength. From here I cannot make head or tail of the political situation in Canada. It seems to me that our country is about to be divided as never before. Such a thing is very deplorable, and those who are encouraging the breach are assuming very grave responsibility."

Currie's only concern was his fighting force.

Smashing barbed wire with trench mortar shells

A German dug-out burning after a hit with phosphorus bombs

The new Canadian commander was proud of his Corps, and he was justifiably pleased to communicate the successes of the Canadian Corps during the remainder of the 1917 campaign.

Engaged in heavy fighting around the Scarpe in April and May, the Canadians fought in the villages of Arleux and Fresnoy before turning towards Lens, the centre of coal production for France.

The troops advanced toward Hill 70, a strategic position.

Taking a short cut through a recently captured village

Haig instructed Currie to concentrate immediately upon taking the city of Lens. Currie decided that Hill 70, one of the two heights dominating the centre, should be the main objective, in that the taking of the hill would give the Allies a tactical advantage from which to pursue Lens.

Hill 70 was Currie's first victory.

The French children as Allies at
Hill 70. August, 1917

"I know you will rejoice with me over the recent successes of our Corps. The fighting for Hill 70 was the hardest and most successful in which we have ever been engaged. Besides gaining ground of great tactical value, we inflicted losses on the enemy which, I am confident, were at least three times those suffered by ourselves. I have never known the Boche to fight so hard and so determinedly before. He counter-attacked us no less than thirty-five times, throwing against us the very best troops in the German army — but all to no avail."

There were 9,198 Canadian casualties, but the Germans lost more, and their casualty figures were estimated at 20,000.

Passchendaele was another costly battle.

Canadian finds his tent and home under water, Vimy Ridge

Two naval guns being removed by Canadian Light Railway, Passchendaele

Between the 26th of October and the 10th of November, 1917, the Allies attacked the village of Passchendaele. Currie had protested that this was too difficult an objective — he forecast 16,000 casualties in its capture.

But Haig insisted. An intense preparatory bombardment ruined the drainage system, and turned No Man's Land into an impossible — almost impassable — bog. Soldiers sunk in the mud up to their knees, and the advance was even more costly than usual.

Canadians gained another victory at Passchendaele.

The Village of Passchendaele and the Goeberg Spur, just to the northwest, were taken in this battle that was among the most costly encounters of the war. Canadians once again underscored their reputation as seasoned, efficient soldiers.

The cost was 15,654 Canadian casualties.

One of the Canadian guns stuck in the mud of Passchendaele

Holding the line. (Machine gunners in shell holes.)

121

Late in 1917, movement became a factor in this war of trenches.

A tank in difficulties

The new land weapon, the tank, had been used ineffectively in the Somme offensive of 1916 and in the mud of Passchendaele.

A major military advance, the new weapon, which would grow into a new arm, required innovations in strategy and tactics that could be evolved only from experience.

The original failures were useful in two senses: the Allies learned that tanks were unsuitable for employment in terrain that was too hilly, and the Germans seriously underestimated the value of the new weapon, and failed to prepare adequate defences.

Sir Julian Byng believed in the ultimate value of the tanks.

Barbed wire stretched across No Man's Land

At Cambrai, in November, 1917, tanks were effectively used in the attack. No advance artillery barrage was necessary. The tanks were able to cut through the defences of No Man's Land and prepare the way for the Infantry advance. The enemy was thus taken by surprise, and a part of the German's defensive Hindenburg Line was smashed.

More secure and manoeuvrable than armoured cars, the tank re-established mobility and speed to what had become a static, defensive war. While the Cavalry distinguished itself at Cambrai as well, it was obviously more vulnerable than the tank.

With the tank, advance was rapid, and entrenched and fortified positions were taken with apparent ease. The Germans were powerless against them, and the role of the tank was assured. Its impact was immense, and Germany concentrated upon developing a tank technology during the interwar period.

The Tank Corps was very popular with Canadians, who were proud of Byng's role in the success of the arm. In 1918, two fully Canadian Tank Battalions were raised.

Armoured trucks on their way to the Front

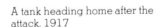

A tank heading home after the attack, 1917

Trial of Canadian 18-pounders against enemy tanks

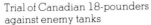

The cost of this war was immense.

Only some of the spent shells
after the Battle of Vimy Ridge,
1917

The defensive positions of the armies of both the Allies and the Central Powers demanded heavy artillery barrage and intense supporting fire for any movement, or planned movement. The routine of these battles meant the expenditure of incredible amounts of munitions. The battle of Valenciennes, for example, accounted for the use of 2,149 tons of ammunition on the first two days of November, 1918: the entire South African campaign had required only 2,800 tons in total.

One estimate noted that all men in the Allied Forces could be fed for less than 7 million dollars per day; a heavy artillery day cost approximately 10 million dollars — to each power!

Munitions not only cost lives and money . . .
They caused scandals at home.

The need for so much ordnance caused incredible growth in the Canadian industrial sector. While it was essential that Canada assume her share of the responsibility for supplying the Allied Forces, it also meant huge profits and potential wealth for those who could find a place in the munitions and war materials industries.

Canadian 18-pounder

Value of munitions and materials exported from Canada.

1914 to December 31	$ 28,164
1915 to December 31	$ 57,213,688
1916 to December 31	$296,505,257
1917 to December 31	$388,213,553
1918 to December 31	$260,711,751
	$1,002,672,413

The shell committee was established in 1914 to rationalize production and supply.

An Honorary Committee, under the Chairmanship of Sam Hughes, was given the responsibility of filling orders for $26,000,000 worth of fuses and shrapnel shell, among other things. The disbursement of these funds prompted the creation of many new companies, and by May, 1915, some four hundred munitions plants were in operation. By November of 1915, orders valued at $300,000,000 had been placed through the Shell Committee, and it was decided that an Imperial Munitions Board, responsible directly to the Imperial Ministry of Munitions, would assume the role of awarding contracts.

In January, 1916, F.B. Carvell, Liberal Member of Parliament for Carleton, New Brunswick, accused the Shell Committee of defrauding Canadian and British taxpayers of millions of dollars through partisan business deals and political favouritism. Carvell presented concrete evidence of scandal, and the country waited for Sir Sam to return from Europe to answer the charges.

Munitions of all sorts — an 1800-pounder and a smaller weapon.

Sam Hughes wasn't worried.

Initially, he simply ignored the details of the charges and informed the country that, "The conduct and operations of the Shell Committee do not come under review by this Parliament." The gravity of the charges prompted an inquiry, but Hughes responded;

"My friends need not worry. My enemies will be dealt with. There is no doubt as to the outcome."

Indeed there wasn't. The convoluted operations of the Shell Committee, and Hughes' trusted lieutenant on that body, Colonel J. Wesley Allison, shocked the Canadian public. Not only was there evidence of political decisions in contract awards — to which Sir Sam replied that there were "no Liberals and no Conservatives in Canada at this time," and therefore no favoritism in the operations of the Shell Committee — but millions of dollars had been awarded to American "mushroom" companies by the Shell Committee. Essentially, the contracts had been given to American entrepreneurs who had a company on paper but no plants, equipment or men at the time of the award. The prices quoted by these Americans were as much as $4.50 per fuse. The same fuses were being made in Canada for $3.50 each.

Hughes responded to these charges that no Canadian company would agree to furnish the required fuses, but the role of the Americans was questioned by many, including the Canadian Manufacturers Association who had evidence that many Canadian companies were prepared to fill orders for munitions. More devastating was the evidence that many of these orders had never been filled, or that faulty munitions had been repeatedly sent, even after initial rejection, to satisfy the contracts.

Soldering fuses in British Munitions Co. Ltd., Verdun

It was incredible to realize that inordinate profits had been made by neutral friends from the blood of Allied soldiers.

The characters of this war, as represented by the troops

The Canadian middlemen, including Allison, accepted "commissions," often very substantial sums, in return for their intercession in assuring a contract. The Americans involved, and some of the less scrupulous Canadian manufacturers, made unprecedented profits through risking and endangering the lives of the men on the front.

Hughes, while he did not make money from his involvement, was held responsible for abusing his Ministerial trust.

There was now a new character in the cast of the First World War: the dangerous dishonesty of supplying the troops had created the role of Profiteer, and money would be inextricably linked with blood as one of the symbols of the First World War.

On December 6, 1917, the city of Halifax was shaken by an explosion in the harbour.

Soldiers engaged in rescue work in Halifax, Nova Scotia

The collision of the munitions ship, *Mont Blanc,* with the Belgian relief ship *Imo* caused an explosion that devastated a large part of the north end of the city and killed an estimated 2,000 people.

The Canadian army was called in to help in the clean-up operation, and the business of munitions left a lasting mark on one Canadian city, which bore a marked resemblance to bombed European cities after the advance.

War needs brought women into the labour force.

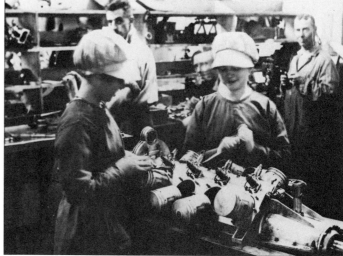

Munitions requirements at the Front prompted constant calls from politicians for more and more production. As manpower requirements increasingly reduced the available labour force, Allied leaders recognized that there was a definite role for women in industrial production and government employment. As one official noted, "The policy of employing women on clerical work connected with the Overseas Military Forces of Canada was governed by the consideration that it released Low Category men employed on clerical work for return to Canada, and the replacement of these men by women clerks further resulted in a considerable saving by the Candian Government."

While women had always fulfilled a role in essential volunteer and medically related services at home, such as the Red Cross, their involvement in the production of essential materials contributed to their credibility as equal citizens. No longer were women restricted to the professional role of nurse, (although even this profession was more fully and responsibly employed in this war) but they became an important aspect of the industrial war which was waged in factories across Canada.

This change of economic role was reflected in women's political role.

The fight for the enfranchisement of women was a multi-levelled affair in Canada, for there was the provincial as well as the federal vote to be won. As the war progressed, many of the provinces extended this right of citizenship to women, although some, like Ontario, would still not allow women to be candidates for membership in their Parliament.

Federal politicians also recognized the contribution of Canada's women, and the first step to achieving complete enfranchisement was taken on this level as well. Sir Robert Borden explained his action in the following words:

"The franchise will be extended to women, not chiefly in recognition of devoted and capable service in the war, but as a measure of justice too long delayed. If men die, women suffer; if they are wounded, women heal; if they are maimed, women labour."

The election of 1917 in which many women did vote would prove that these glowing words and actions were more political than sincere, but the step, once taken, could not be retraced. Shortly after the war, women won the unqualified right to vote in federal elections.

Women had always fought against booze.

Prohibition Parade, Toronto,
Ontario, March 8, 1916

The war gave added impact to the temperance crusade, and the fight against booze became an aspect of the First World War that affected everyone on the domestic front.

"We are fighting Germany, Austria, and drink, and so far as I can see the greatest of these three deadly forces is drink."

Lloyd George, 1915

Canadians were inclined to agree, and diminished industrial output due to excessive drinking became an explanation for many failures to meet deadlines and obligations. The availability of liquor to the soldier had been regulated early in the war, and owners of drinking establishments were bound to curtail the hours during which they would serve men in uniform. But the need for munitions and the requirement for constant production prompted the Allied governments to become more concerned about the availability of alcohol to civilians. In 1916 the French government announced that any munitions worker caught drinking would be sent to the Front. Canada's provinces passed laws that limited distillation, importation, distribution and sale of intoxicating liquor (anything with an alcohol content of more than 2.5 per cent); the most comprehensive and final act being passed by the federal government in 1918.

Prohibition was thus total, but it did not last much longer than the war.

While the popular movement for prohibition concentrated on the destructive potential of alcohol and its abuses by the labouring classes, there was also concern about the amount of grain used to produce alcohol. This, in turn, was a part of one of the growing issues of the war: Food — production, supply, and cost.

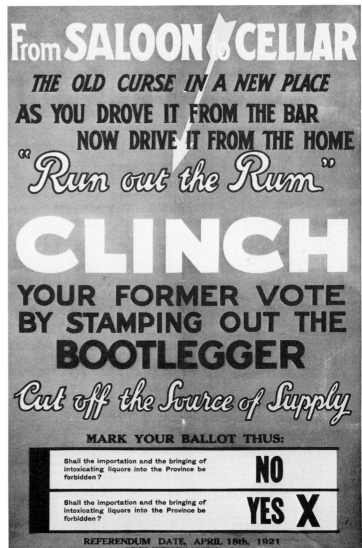

Starvation was an ally — when it was Germany that suffered.

Food shortages in Germany were reported as early as 1915, and constant mention of bread riots and starving cities were hopeful signs to Allied readers. One newspaper editor estimated that with each discharge of a 75-mile gun, the Germans spent $5,000, killed an average of one French mother and child by shell-fire, and a dozen German mothers and children by starvation.

But more than the possibility of starving Germany into Peace, the Canadians felt gravely the weight of their responsibility to keep their Allies fed:

"The outstanding fact of the food situation, which it is imperative that every citizen of Canada should realize at once, is that Great Britain, France, Italy, Belgium, and their European allies are wholly unable to supply the Allied armies at the Front and on the way. For nearly three years their manpower has been engaged in the direct work of the war, and in some cases large areas of their most productive lands have been overrun by the enemy. Their food shortage and the food to supply the armies . . . must be wholly provided from this side of the Atlantic."

Hon. W.J. Hanna,
Food Controller, 1917

Europe's food shortage was aggravated by the wanton destruction of farms and land in the German retreat. Here, every tree in an orchard is sawn in half.

Canadian cook making a small oven in the support lines, September, 1917

The troops had to eat also.

Canadian military authorities were well aware of the need to keep troops well fed, and while Canadians enjoyed their share of "hardtack" and "bully," the usually unpalatable bread and meat military ration, efforts were made to ensure that meals of sufficient quality and quantity were provided whenever possible.

Cooks were trained to operate under conditions at the Front, and the Canadian diet was supplemented with frozen fish flown in three times weekly, as well as the usual packages from home and Christmas gifts of food.

"We are saving you, YOU save FOOD"

Well fed Soldiers WILL WIN the WAR

There were profiteers among the food suppliers too.

Feeding the soldiers — the need for wheat

In November, 1915, the federal government announced, without warning, that it was commandeering fifteen million bushels of wheat. Attempts to buy grain on the open market the previous year had prompted speculators to enter the market-place and greatly disarrange the commodity exchange. Wheat, however, was an essential product, and the government argued that in commandeering the product they were penalizing only the middlemen who were missing an opportunity to make fast profits.

There was a pork scandal as well. Extremely high profits enjoyed by Sir Joseph Flavelle's meat packing company, especially in bacon production, prompted an investigation. The revelation that Flavelle's company had made five million dollars in 1916 alone from this product gave rise to the institution of the position of Food Controller in 1917. Increasingly, supplies and prices were controlled, and legislation against hoarding was passed to control even the individual. In a very profound sense, Canada felt herself responsible — (more so than the other colonies who were too far away for transport purposes) for ensuring an adequate supply of food to her Allies and her troops.

Poster: Canada's Egg Opportunity

In every detail of the Canadian economy, war meant increased volume.

The conflict meant a vast expansion of exports in all sorts of commodities, as well as increased government purchasing. The average value of Canadian exports during 1912, 1913 and 1914 was $188,958,091. Trade in the same products in 1918 totalled $833,389,047.

Canadian businessmen had recognized that the dislocation in world trade would create a situation favourable to them, and the question they asked themselves was whether they could rise to the demands and accept control of some of the trade lost by Germany and Austria. In that 1914 was a year of recession and drought, and the dismal economic realities that came with such events, the war had been a fortuitous answer to the economic distress of Canadian entrepreneurs. Moreover, Canadian businessmen perceived the change as a permanent reorganization of the world economy: the end of the war would sustain the boom, for while the rest of the industrialized world recovered, Canada could take full advantage of her favoured geography and continue to supply European needs.

Vancouver Engineering Works, 1915

Completely black horses at the
Front line

As with munitions and food, certain sectors of private enterprise proved inadequate to the moral demands of wartime trade. From the very first year of the hostilities, Canadian politicians and businessmen were involved in scandals of varying degrees that were the result of supplying everything from drugs to

horses. Government inquiries into war purchases revealed amazing profits and unscrupulous business practices that more often than not involved a combination of Canadian and American business-men and politicians.

The politicians (or their secretaries, assistants, or friends) accepted commissions for arrang-ing contracts, a business practice that was open to severe abuse. And many were willing to go to dangerous extremes, such as painting white horses black in order to meet military requirements that stated no white markings were acceptable, to make their money.

The Conservative party, whose ranks were rife with participants in these frauds and scandals, abjured any responsibility for their existence. Members who were caught were asked to resign, but Prime Minister Borden advised the public that "Enormous purchases had to be made in [a] short time. Improprieties and fraud which occurred were in violation of express Ministerial orders."

These scandalous deals only increased the cost of the war for the Canadian citizen.

Under the special powers enjoyed by the government during wartime, the Conservative budgets successively increased taxes on luxury goods and services, such as phonographs and steamer tickets, as well as certain financial arrangements. But in July 1917, Sir Thomas White, the Minister of Finance, announced a graduated Income Tax that was to be implemented in Canada. The incomes of unmarried men were taxed at a rate of four per cent when they exceeded $2,000, while married men with dependents were taxed at the same rate when over $3,000. Additional taxes were charged on incomes over $6,000 at an increasing rate up to twenty-five per cent, which was the assessment rate levied against personal incomes in excess of $100,000. This measure was announced as a temporary assessment.

The complaints about this legislation focussed not on the idea of the tax, but on what was perceived to be the unfair distribution of the rate of taxation in which the low income earner was burdened more than the wealthy individual. Also, in view of wartime trade conditions, the excess profits that had been revealed were still taxed at four per cent — the rate of tax levied against business incomes over $3,000.

One of the toughest battles was financial.

The enemy's aggression had to be met, shell for shell, and money was constantly solicited to support this trust. The Victory Loan campaign annually informed the civilian public of the cost of the war and of the part they could play in achieving victory. A contribution to the Victory Loan could feed or equip a soldier: $1,000, for example, could pay the wages of 1,000 soldiers for one day; buy 200 pairs of boots; buy 450 bushels of wheat; buy 100 sets of infantry equipment, 2,000 pounds of high explosives; or 200 gas masks that could save 200 soldiers' lives. Surely this was not much to give up some luxuries for! And the contributions were tax deductible.

Victory Loan Parade, Montreal, 1917. A British Tank on Sherbrooke St.

Canadian J.N. 4 Machine used by Canadian Aeroplanes Ltd. in Victory Loan Parade

The families of men overseas required support, as well.

The circumstances of the formation of the Canadian Expeditionary Force had been so rushed, so immediate, that the wives and children of serving men were frequently left without adequate support. The Canadian Patriotic Fund was founded under the auspices of the Governor-General, the Duke of Connaught. This organization provided for the families of Canadian soldiers who found themselves in need. When the government recognized their responsibility in this area, and provided for the transfer of money to dependents, the Patriotic Fund formed a plan for supplementing incomes. Adjustments were made to ensure that women with dependents were fairly supported in comparison with women who had no dependents, and care was taken that those unscrupulous women who married soldiers on the way to the Front in an attempt to secure themselves an income for the duration were discovered. While some abuse of this sort was undoubtedly successful, the administrators of the Patriotic Fund were careful and conscientious, and the organization filled a necessary role in the total war effort.

145

One need eclipsed all others — Men were essential.

Recruiting continued at a quick pace throughout the war in an attempt to satisfy Allied demands for men. But the Canadian tradition of volunteer enlistment was adhered to by Borden and Laurier who insisted that compulsory military service was not appropriate to the Canadian war effort even when various civilian groups began agitating for conscription.

Compulsory enlistment had become a more fully implemented policy in Great Britain in December, 1915, when "single slackers" were forced to enlist. By May, 1916 there was compulsory military service in Britain.

In January 1917 Sir Robert Borden returned from a visit to the Front convinced of the real need for more men in the struggle to triumph over Germany. Lloyd George, the most forceful of European leaders, had argued convincingly the urgency of immediate reinforcements. In Europe, the sentiment was unanimously in favour of compulsion; the voluntary principle had ceased to provide men.

Conscription was not a new idea in Canada.

Recruits lining up on Station Street, Toronto, Ontario

While the politicians had argued the appropriateness of voluntary enlistment principle in Canada, many Canadian citizens, both individually and in groups, had suggested the logic of conscription. Indeed, it was perceived to be a rational method of ensuring a constant supply of men, and a sensible allocation of expertise and ability, both at home and in Europe.

The atmosphere was uncomfortable for any man who remained at home. No matter how many hours or dollars were given in support of the war, the man who served on the home front was frequently treated as a slacker or a coward and constantly laboured under social pressure to account for the fact that he was not in uniform, and still in Canada. It was felt that this unhealthy atmosphere would disappear if a selective system of compulsory registration and enlistment were implemented.

Until the winter of 1917 Borden rejected the idea of compulsory service. He and his Liberal counterpart, Laurier, had persistently advocated the viability of the voluntary principle; Borden had rejected citizens' arguments until the Russian collapse on the Eastern Front, coupled with Lloyd George's insistence, convinced him of the need for compulsory military service. And once converted to this idea, Borden was convinced of its necessity.

Many Canadian groups opposed compulsion.

Henri Bourassa, 1912

The most obvious, most famous and most long-lived division was between French and English. The announcement of the Military Service Bill was greeted with knowing alarm in Quebec: the French Canadians had been warned by Henri Bourassa and his Nationalist followers of the implications and dangers of Imperialism. The idea that each little involvement lead to a larger, more devastating commitment, seemed justified in June 1917, especially in terms of other events that appeared to threaten French Canada within the context of Confederation. The recruitment policies of Sam Hughes had exacerbated cultural tensions, and the passage of Regulation 17 in Ontario, an Act that appeared to herald the death of French education in the neighbour province, placed Borden's policy in a context that exaggerated the severity of its cultural implications.

Laurier promised his co-operation, but he would not betray his promises. He demanded a referendum as proof of public enthusiasm for the policy, and argued that not only manpower, but wealth, should be conscripted by the government in the name of the war effort. These suggestions were discounted, even ridiculed, by English Canadian proponents of the policy; the sheer weight of their numbers overcame Laurier's suggestions.

"I oppose this Bill because it has in it the seeds of discord and disunion; because it is an obstacle and a bar to that union of heart and soul without which it is impossible to hope that this Confederation will attain the aims and ends that were had in view when Confederation was effected."

Sir Wilfrid Laurier

ONE WHO IS PLEASED

THE KAISER:-"HOCH DER LAURIER POLICY! IF HE WINS THERE WILL BE NO MORE CANADIANS TO WORRY ME" VOTE - UNION - GOVERNMENT

For Canada, conscription meant an election.

The internal divisions that resulted from this legislation dictated a political contest, rather than another mutually-acceptable extension of Parliament. Even before the need for an election was generally accepted, Borden and the Conservatives were working to ensure their continued political influence. The idea that there was no room in the war effort for less than total unity was extended to mean that there was no room for political parties or choice on the Canadian scene.

In October, 1917, Borden announced the formation of a Union Government. This was represented as symbolizing a sense of national unity and purpose, a healthy desire to win the war without division. But the Cabinet of this government included prominent English Canadian Liberals — A.L. Sifton, premier of Alberta; T.A. Crerar, Manitoba agricultural expert; N.W. Rowell, Ontario Liberal Leader and C.C. Ballantyne and Hugh Guthrie, eastern Liberals — without similar representation from French Canada. It was this united, patriotic, and English group that entered the election campaign, armed fully and vocally with the weapons of unity and duty.

Your Chums are fighting

Why aren't YOU?

If there was no room for parties, there was plenty of scope for politics.

THE FIDDLER

NERO "FIDDLING" WITH POLITICS WHILE THE FLAMES SPREAD

VOTE - UNION - GOVERNMENT

The Military Voters Act of mid-August, 1917, gave the vote to all soldiers enlisted in the Canadian forces no matter what their citizenship or period of residency in the Dominion.

The Wartime Elections Act of September, 1917, enfranchised all women (mothers, wives, sisters, daughters) related to Canadian service men, and disenfranchised all people who had immigrated from alien countries since 1902, whether naturalized citizens or not.

The most useful electoral legislation was the Military Voters act, which enfranchised all military personnel, male and female, and which gave the government rather excessive ability to gerrymander. Soldiers were asked to vote for either the Government or the Opposition, and if they could not identify their home ridings the electoral officer was empowered to assign their votes. This provision was useful in deciding contested seats.

The Union Government attacks Laurier.

A VOTE FOR A UNIONIST CANDIDATE IS A VOTE FOR REINFORCEMENTS. The Union Government is pledged to carry on its work of raising the 100,000 reinforcements so urgently needed to support the Canadians at the Front. Laurier and his adherents would stop this work, take a referendum, and experiment with voluntary enlistment, the possibilities of which have been exhausted. The most clear-headed, right-minded Liberals have gladly and without coercion helped to form the Union Government; they have weighed the pros and cons, they have not allowed politics to interfere with their patriotism, or their promise to our brave boys in France to "see them through."

Union Government
Advertisement

Electioneering at a Canadian
hospital overseas

153

There was little doubt as to how the majority of serving men would vote.

Canadians voting up the line, December, 1917

At home, Borden pursued an anti-Laurier campaign that was buttressed by constant reference to the need for additional men on the Western Front. While Borden subscribed to the belief that if the Allies could keep pouring men into the fight they would ultimately wear Germany down, his insistence upon the necessity of conscription (which was intimately tied to the victory of the Union Government under his leadership) was questioned by General Currie. The leader of the Canadian Corps was more concerned that a Fifth Canadian Division, under the command of Lieutenant-General Garnet Hughes, son of Sir Sam Hughes, was held in England when it might be reinforcing Canadian Divisions on the Front. For this reason, he refused to comply with Conservative demands that he transmit messages to the Canadian public that might have strengthened Borden's credibility.

The Union Government won an outstanding victory, and only Quebec returned a significant number of opposition candidates. This election provided the tangible evidence of the profound alienation of French Canada and reinforced a tradition, that went back to Riel, of antipathy toward the Conservative party on the part of Quebec voters.

Conscription's impact was more emotional than real.

In January, 1918, M. J.N. Francoeur of the Quebec House moved: "We believe the time has come either to stop these sterile quarrels or to accept their logical consequences. To the detractors of Quebec this resolution means that if the Province is in the way of Confederation, it is ready to talk the thing over...." Within a week, the resolution had been withdrawn, and Premier Lomer Gouin was reiterating the argument that Confederation was the only form of government suitable for Quebec, or Canada; but the conscription question in the First World War did much to increase Quebec's sense of regional identity as a unique component within the Canadian context.

This signal of discontent was followed by active demonstrations of Quebec's unhappiness, and riots and demonstrations sometimes reached levels of unprecedented violence.

But it was not only French Canadians who objected to conscription. Farmers and organized labour were not convinced of the absolute necessity of this legislation — and if their rejection of the policy was less obvious and not so fully reported, they were equally as strong. There were incidents of violence and disrupted meetings in other regions, and Borden was called upon more than once to deal with delegations of English-speaking objectors.

Anti-conscription demonstration, Victoria Square, Montreal

In the end, the numbers were less than significant.

Over 400,000 men registered under the Act. Of these, 379,629 requested exemption: 112,625 were declared unfit to serve; 222,364 were granted exemptions; and 59,991 were ordered to report for duty. Of the men made available by this Act, Quebec accounted for 55,814 and Ontario for 55,145. Of both groups, most were farmers. And Canadians were hard pressed to assess the real necessity and validity of the conscription policy.

The United States finally declared war.

"American Legion" soldiers on University Avenue, Toronto. January 7, 1915

The United States maintained its status as a neutral until April of 1917. There had been many incidents of more than sufficient gravity to prompt a declaration of war, but President Wilson had avoided the issue and maintained the precious neutrality that was also profitable. For the United States became the banker of this war, and even the experience of the *Lusitania*, infamous symbol of German depravity, did not interrupt the flow of loans and manufactures to the Allies.

American men did volunteer, however, and the 97th Overseas Battalion was popularly known as the "American Legion." Complaints from the government of the United States about the use of the word "American" caused it to be dropped from the official description — but the soldiers still used the name.

It was commercial pressure that finally convinced the United States.

Balfour, Joffre and Viviani, the
Allied representatives, at Mount
Vernon, April, 1917

From the early months of the war the neutral powers had felt the effects of naval blockades, both by the Allies and the Central Powers. The United States continually protested the interruption of their trade, but the engaged powers did not alter their policies.

"The head of a great nation, whatever his private views may be ... must adopt a neutral attitude. America is far removed from the horrors of this war. We are in the midst of them. America is neutral; we are not neutral. We believe that the essence of this conflict is a question which is as old as time — the difference between right and wrong. We believe, we know, that this is a war of naked aggression; that crimes which have accompanied the conduct of the war, which have been unknown in the world for centuries, are small in comparison with the initial crime of plunging the world into war by cold-blooded calculation because those responsible thought it would pay."

Andrew Bonar Law, 1917

By 1917, the effects of Germany's submarine blockade were deemed intolerable, and the United States declared a state of armed neutrality, and then war against Germany. Canadian officers were promptly sent south to aid in training troops that under General Pershing would enter the war on the Western Front later that year.

The story of American participation in the First World War is one of contradiction. They were perceived as saviours by many members of the Allied leadership — but their neutrality had become impossible by 1917. While they had shared in the profits of this war, they had experienced none of the real burdens between 1914 and 1917. If their contribution was substantial, it was relatively much less significant than Canada's, a statistic that applied to casualties as well. Understandably, Canadians who had served in Europe since 1915 were annoyed when American troops were assigned to their ships for the return trip in 1919.

Wilson was an idealist. His country's neutrality underscored his respectability as a peacemaker in this war; and his humanistic rhetoric appealed to those Allied commanders who had been arguing for years that theirs was the ultimate battle for the preservation of civilization. But the President was not the nation.

Canadian and American Officers meet in France, October, 1917

Canadians won increased military independence as the 1918 campaign began.

"Three Cheers and a Tiger" for
Sir Robert Borden

In July, 1918 Canadian control of her overseas forces was once again improved through the formation of a Canadian Section of the General Headquarters of the British Armies in France. Not only did this reorganization ensure a fuller involvement of the Canadian government in the administration of Canadian forces overseas, it accorded Canada the status of a nation in the military bureaucracy. It was an important and portentous step in the history of Canada's Imperial relations, and the Canadians thus entered the campaign of 1918 more united, more fully integrated, than ever before in this war.

But the war still had not been won.

The first major engagement of 1918 was the Battle of Amiens, August 8-11, 1918. This was preceded by the Charge of Flowerdew's Squadron, a Cavalry action in which the knights of the twentieth century distinguished themselves.

(No. 8571) Charge of Flowerdew's Squadron. Oil on canvas by Sir Alfred Munnings

Americans had entered the line.

But it was the Canadians who were chosen to spearhead the attack.

"The Canadians played a part of such distinction that thenceforward they were marked out as storm troops; for the remainder of the war they were brought along to head the assault in one great battle after another. Whenever the Germans found the Canadian Corps coming into the line they prepared for the worst."

Lloyd George, 1916

Canadians advancing during
Amiens, August, 1918

This was the role that Canadians played at Amiens.

Currie misled the Germans with a mock attack on the city of Arras but moved his troops back to Amiens for an attack made jointly with the Australians that was a brilliant success.

The Germans lost 27,000 men and 400 guns. But more important, the German High Command experienced a severe crisis of confidence.

Currie immediately turned to Arras.

The advance east of Arras,
August, 1918

The Second Battle of
Arras lasted from 26
August through 3
September, 1918.
Canadian troops fought
their way through three
extremely strong lines of
defence as far as the
Canal du Nord, where
they paused to wait for the
advance of other Allied
troops.

Tanks were again used
in this offensive, and their
status as a permanent
(and important) arm was
established beyond a
doubt.

"There were tanks — so
my company surrendered
— I also," was how one
German officer described
the encounter.

The attack was pushed forward.

A German giving himself up

The Canal du Nord

The Canal du Nord and Cambrai were the objects of attack from 27 September, 1918, on. Canadians crossed the Canal du Nord on 27 September, and reached Cambrai on 9 October.

The Germans had devastated Cambrai in preparation for the entrance of Allied troops.

As Currie described the scene:

"Cambrai was to be deliberately set on fire by the enemy. Huge fires were burning in the Square when our patrols went through, and many others broke out in all parts of the city. Piles of inflammable material were found ready for the torch, but the enemy was unable to carry out his intention owing to our unexpected attack and rapid progress."

This advance liberated 116 square miles of French soil and some 54 towns and villages, including Cambrai.

Over Cambrai, 1918

The Germans withdrew to the Hermann Line.

At Valenciennes the Canadians encountered German troops in their last defensive line. A village dominated by Mont Houy, Valenciennes was taken on the first two days of November, 1918.

As the first Allied soldiers to enter the town in almost four years, Canadians were welcomed as liberators and friends.

An elaborate Ferro concrete trap erected by Germans to arrest the advance of Allied tanks

Then it was on to Mons.

On November 10-11th, Canadians entered the village of Mons. It was here that the British had first engaged the Germans in August 1914. And so it was here that the troops waited for peace, fighting until late on the tenth in anticipation of the armistice.

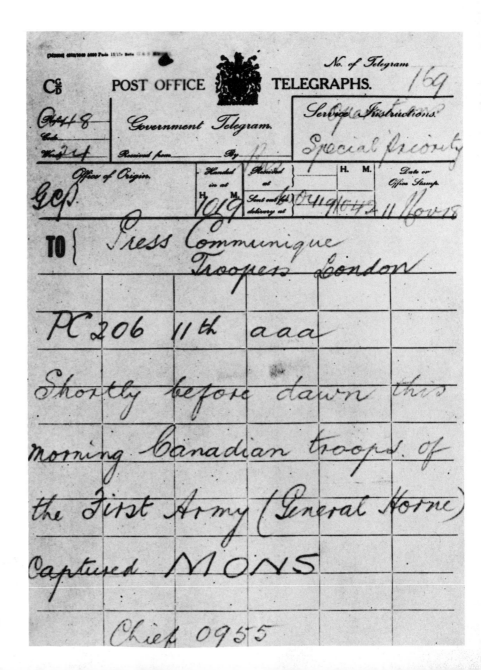

Copy of last Press Telegram regarding capture of Mons, November 11, 1918

The cease-fire on the Western Front was set for the eleventh hour of the eleventh day of the eleventh month.

As one Canadian soldier described the experience:

"I was standing on the slope of the hill. I could see Mons on my left. I could hear the bands playing. I could hear the people cheering and shouting and all the rejoicing in the village behind, but out front it was just dead silence and we really couldn't believe it. That's my reaction. The troops in action and I went up to the front line immediately afterward and there was certainly no elation, no rejoicing, they wanted to go to bed. It was the end and they just couldn't realize it. Came so suddenly."

Armistice message received by wireless at 5th Canadian Artillery Headquarters, November 11, 1918

Celebrating the Armistice,
Toronto, November 7, 1918

The war was over on the Western Front.

German Officers fly white flag when entering Canadian lines to show where mines were laid by their engineers, November, 1918

It remained to find out where the Germans had laid their munitions traps; liberate the conquered parts of Belgium and France; and occupy Germany, to ensure that no future conflict would be given birth in that nation.

Canadian soldiers were legally members of the Militia involved in Home Defence. As such, they could not be committed to unlimited employment in Europe; but they did participate in the March to the Rhine, where General Currie took the salute at Bonn simultaneously with Sir Herbert Plumer who reviewed at Cologne.

Currie was proud, concerned, and reassuring in these days of undefined peace:

"Some of you have already commenced, while others are about to march on the Rhine, liberating Belgium in your advance. In a few days you will enter Germany and hold certain parts, in order to secure the fulfilment of the terms of the armistice preliminary to the peace treaty. The rulers of Germany, humiliated and demoralized, have fled. That unscrupulous nation, who in 1914 set at naught every treaty and violated every moral obligation . . . is beaten, famished and at our mercy. Justice has come. Retribution commences.

"During four long years, conscious of the righteousness of your cause, you have fought many battles and endured cruel hardships, and now your mighty efforts are rewarded. Your comrades are avenged. . . .

"Rest assured that the crimes of Germany will receive adequate punishment. Attempts will be made by insidious propaganda to undermine the source of your strength, but you, the soldier citizens of the finest and most advanced democracy in the world, will treat such attempts with the contempt they deserve. You know that self-imposed, stern discipline has made you the hardest, most successful and cleanest fighters of this war. Beginning by the immortal stand at the second battle of Ypres, you befittingly closed by the capture of Mons your fighting record, in which every battle you fought is a resplendent page of glory. I trust you, and the memory of your dead comrades demands of you to bring back that glorious record pure and unsullied to Canada."

Canadians crossing the Rhine at
Bonn

A Canadian pacifies a little Belgian baby near Mons, whose mother was killed by an enemy shell; the child was wounded in its mother's arms, November, 1918.

Passing through Valenciennes

Canadian transport drivers assisting French refugees who are returning to their homes after the armistice, November, 1918

The German flag which was taken down from the Hôtel de Ville, Valenciennes, November, 1918

This was the end of the war of 1914-18. There was still a war of 1919.

Canadians with Russian women transport drivers, February, 1919

Allied victory on most fronts had secured the ultimate conclusion of hostilities on the Western Front: the British had smashed the Turks in Syria; Bulgaria had been neutralized by the Salonika campaign; and on October 4, 1918, the German and Austrian governments had asked President Wilson to negotiate an armistice based upon bilateral conditions.

There was still a campaign in Northern Russia.

Eighteen-pounder gun being hauled through the snow in Northern Russia, 1919

There was a Canadian presence in Siberia and along the coast of Russia. While Russia had been an important ally throughout most of the war, the Eastern Front had collapsed in the wake of an internal Revolution, and Lenin had signed the Treaty of Brest-Litovsk with Germany and disrupted the Allied structure. The Allies, however, were concerned that the Pacific Coast be guarded against the establishment of German submarine ports, and it was for this specific reason that Canadian troops were dispatched to northern Russia.

The political situation in Russia changed drastically in a relatively short period of time, and the Canadians found themselves in an anomalous role. Rather than fighting the Germans, they became a part of the Siberian population's struggle to hold off the Bolsheviks. Thus it was the Canadians were active champions of the White Russians.

Canadians did not play a decisive role in Northern Russia.

The engagements that were experienced were handled extremely well, however, and the White Russian government awarded ten Saint George's Crosses and ten Saint George's Medals to the troops. According to Russian custom, the medals were granted to the twenty bravest men as decided by their comrades.

Prime Minister Borden was convinced that the Canadian presence was essential for her international prestige and reputation. But by the spring of 1919, public opinion was running against the war, and the troops were called home.

Demobilization was a massive task.

Lunch at an Estaminet,
Mericourt, 1919

Leaving Belgium for Le Havre
and home, March, 1919

Canadian troops were involved in occupation duties until February 1919 when the real job of repatriation began.

Numerous sorts of financial benefits were arranged — a gratuity, assisted loans, and pensions were instituted in an attempt to re-establish the veteran. Indeed, Veterans Affairs became an active and important aspect of the Canadian Military establishment because of this experience.

The repatriation of the soldier and his personal reintegration into North American society were supported by both government and civilian groups such as the Y.M.C.A.

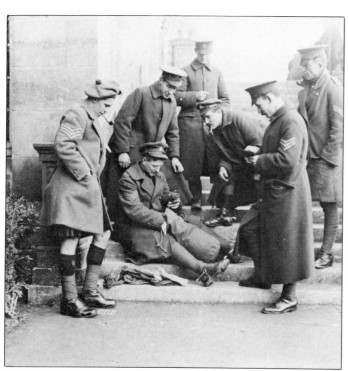

Packing his kit at the Canadian
Discharge Depot

Dominion troops parading
through London on their way
home, May, 1919

Memorials

Memorial to Canadian Artillery,
Vimy Ridge. General Sir Arthur
Currie is in front.

Impossible as it was to memorialize the Canadian sacrifice, a government committee dealt with the creation of suitable graves and memorials. Wherever possible, isolated graves were amalgamated into larger cemeteries where uniform headstones, with no distinction as to rank or status, marked the death.

When no bodies were found, memorials were erected.

181

The Allies had to create a peace.

(No. 8796) The Flag. Oil on Canvas by J.B.L. Shaw

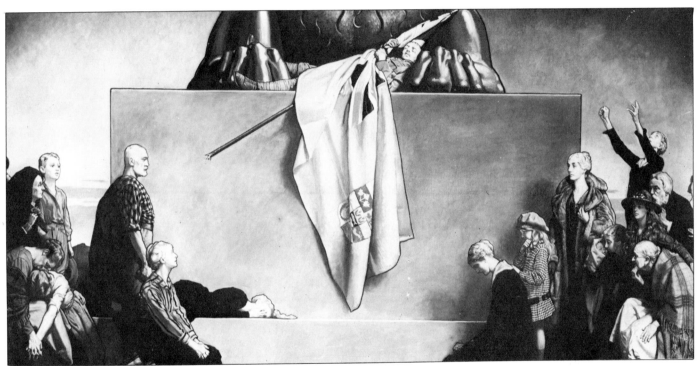

Étaples, France

These had been years of unequalled violence and horror, involving to an extent that would have been unthinkable two decades earlier. The moral imperative that sustained the Allied Powers in their struggle also intensified their expectations of peace.

Both the Pope and President Wilson had presented peace proposals during the war. But all mediators were treated to the same response: there was no room in this war for a negotiated peace. Unconditional surrender was the only way to end the conflict, and Germany had to be taught a lesson. There must be no possibility of rearming the menace; there must be restitution for damage and injury.

Once again, it was Germany that was the enemy; Austria-Hungary and Turkey were merely losers. And the conquest for civilization was a victory over Germany's militarism, imperialism and nationalism.

Canada had a role to play in that decision.

Victoria Cross Winners, August 28, 1920

This nation of barely eight million people had provided a fighting force of unequalled ability, reputation and discipline. Military honours and Allied medals were impressive in their quantity, and Canada created her own symbols of service.

Thus, a part of the Canadian legacy was a military reputation. The volunteer militia had proved itself one of the exceptional fighting organizations of the world.

There was an international identity to be established.

Allies around the Peace Table,
Paris, 1919

The peace negotiations, where the world map was redrawn, along moral, not physical lines, was important to Canada. While the Americans and French objected to the separate presence of the Dominion at the peace talks, Lloyd George successfully convinced Woodrow Wilson of Canada's right to participation in these decisions in light of her more than significant contribution to the total effort. Canada thus appeared at the treaty negotiations and was granted a separate seat in the League of Nations when it was formed.

This was a new concept of Canadian nationality.

Made more piquant by memories of the deep regional divisions caused by conscription, the end of the fighting prompted a close sense of nationhood, the bond increased by a new sense of military traditions, and co-operation. As one soldier commented:

"I've always thought that the Canadian nation was, in fact, born on the battlefields of Europe. I'm sure that that's true, that the fierce pride developed in the Canadians in their own identity, in their own nationhood, was a very real thing, and it survived over into the peace. Whenever they give the Canadians a chance to show their identity or to be proud of their identity, they are, and they always rise to the occasion."

Showing the flag

This was complemented by a boom economic mentality.

Canada had grown through this war. It was an industrialized, modern economic unit, and businessmen had no intention of slacking off just because the war was over.

While many young men had to be re-integrated into the job market, there was an overwhelming sense of security and optimism that characterized the Canadian business community, which had begun to prepare for peace many years prior to the actual event.

Canada's was an economy that was more and more closely coming under the scrutiny, and even the control, of the government. One aspect of the legacy of the war would be the continuation of a major economic role for the federal government.

The political legacy of the First World War had its positive aspects — the right of Canadian women to vote in federal elections — as well as its negative. Memories of scandals, and the dangerous experience of conscription, had called into question some of the bases of the Canadian political system. A Union Government of racially-defined politicians had doomed the real political co-operation administered by Laurier of 1914-17. As the fighting men returned and renewed their acquaintance with Canada, many questions were left unanswered.

Organized labour and farmers, who had been slighted by the Conservatives in their decision to enforce conscription, would also focus their criticisms. And the war that was fought to ensure a moral peace would foster a period of dissent and protest in Canada, both urban and rural.

And for the men who had fought, there were memories . . . nightmares . . . of Flanders.

After it was over, the incredible reality of this war began to penetrate. There were curses for the politicians and generals, and revulsion at the inhuman conflict which had continued for so long.

This was a haunted victory that would not last, for the Peace for Civilization cultivated the ground for another, more efficient war in which the inventions and strategies of the First World War would be brought into more deadly play.

(No. 8120) Death Tolls Again over Flanders. Etching by Jules De Bruyker

What would follow: urban and rural protest; regional growth. And there were endless images of Flanders.

While Canadians had
fought in other theatres
during this First World
War, it was the powerful
images of Flanders that
haunted their victory.

Bent double, like old beggars under sacks,
Knock-kneed, coughing like hags, we cursed through sludge,
Till on the haunting flares we turned our backs
And towards our distant rest began to trudge.
Men marched asleep. Many had lost their boots
But limped on, blood-shod. All went lame; all blind;
Drunk with fatigue, deaf even to the hoots
Of tired, oustripped Five-Nines that dropped behind.

Gas! Gas! Quick, boys!—An ecstasy of fumbling,
Fitting the clumsy helmets just in time;
But someone still was yelling out and stumbling
And flound'ring like a man in fire or lime . . .
Dim, through the misty panes and thick green light,
As under a green sea, I saw him drowning.

In all my dreams, before my helpless sight,
He plunges at me, guttering, choking, drowning.

If in some smothering dreams you too could pace
Behind the wagon that we flung him in,
And watch the white eyes writhing in his face,
His hanging face, like a devil's sick of sin;
If you could hear, at every jolt, the blood
Come gargling from the froth-corrupted lungs,
Obscene as cancer, bitter as the cud
Of vile, incurable sores on innocent tongues,—
My friend, you would not tell with such high zest
To children ardent for some desperate glory,
The old Lie: Dulce et decorum est
Pro patria mori.

Wilfred Owen

Further Reading

There is a multitude of volumes that deal with the First World War, ranging in scope from regimental histories or tactical studies to multi-volume chronicles of the Imperial experience. One need only browse through the military history area of any library to discover interesting and revealing material for further reading. Two general histories, which are different and complementary, are Captain B.H. Liddell Hart's *The Real War 1914-1918* (Toronto, 1964) and A.J.P. Taylor's *The First World War: An Illustrated History* (Norfolk, 1977). Both are written from the perspective of the involvement of the major powers, the former being an informed military account and the latter a very sensitive portrait of the human and political experience of the First World War.

Canada's experience in this War is gradually becoming a more fully described part of our historical literature. Two official histories have been written: Colonel A. Fortescue Duguid's *History of the Canadian Forces 1914-19* (Ottawa, 1938) and Colonel G.W.L. Nicholson's *Canadian Expeditionary Force 1914-1919* (Ottawa, 1962). D.H. Goodspeed's *The Road Past Vimy: The Canadian Corps 1914-1918* (Toronto, 1969) is an extremely readable and informative account, and J.A. Swettenham's book, *Canada and the First World War* (Toronto, 1969) is an excellent introduction to the sequence of Canadian participation in the War. For more precise information as to army organization and operations two official documents, *Canada's Part in the Great War* and the *Report of the Ministry, Overseas Military Forces of Canada, 1918* are useful.

The issues of the War in Canada are dealt with in more general texts as well. G.F.G. Stanley's *Canada's Soldiers: The Military History of an Unmilitary People, 1604-1954,* (Toronto, 1954) reveals the growth of the Canadian forces, and the conscription issue is dealt with by J.L. Granatstein and J.M. Hitsman in *Broken Promises: A History of Conscription in Canada* (Toronto, 1977). One of the finest comprehensive accounts of the period may be found in *Canada 1896-1921: A Nation Transformed* (Toronto, 1974) by R. Craig Brown and Ramsay Cook.

All of these works are complemented by an original source that is generally available: the contemporary newspaper. Almost any issue of a major Canadian paper will reveal a number of aspects of the dramatic changes that Canadians experienced during the period 1914-18, and it is worth a Saturday afternoon at the library to enlarge one's perception of the variety of experiences the First World War represented.

191

INDEX

'Dulce et Decorum Est" from *The Collected Poems of Wilfred Owen* edited by C. Day Lewis (copyright 1946, © 1963 by Chatto & Windus, Ltd.) is reprinted by permission of Chatto & Windus, the Executors of the Estate of Harold Owen, and New Directions Publishing Corporation.

All photographs courtesy of the *Public Archives of Canada*, Ottawa, except for the following: *The Canadian War Museum*, 42, 71, 95, 110, 161, 183, 189. *Queen's University Archives*, 43.

Map entitled *The Western Front in Outline 1914-1918* is reprinted with permission of Heinemann Educational Books Ltd.; from the book *A Military Atlas of the First World War* by Arthur Banks.

The publisher has made every effort to give accurate credit to the sources of quotations and illustrations which appear in this book. In the event of error or omission, notification would be appreciated.